Healing Prayers

Healing Prayers

Clift & Kathleen
RICHARDS

Victory House, Inc.
Tulsa, Oklahoma

Unless otherwise indicated, all Scripture quotations are taken from the *King James Version* of the Bible.

Scripture quotations marked NKJV are taken from *The New King James Version,* copyright 1982 by Thomas Nelson, Inc. used by permission.

Prayers and meditations are paraphrased from these versions unless otherwise stated.

Healing Prayers
Copyright © 2002 by F. Clift and Kathleen Richards
ISBN 0-932081-75-4

Published by Victory House, Inc.
P.O. Box 700238
Tulsa, Oklahoma 74170
(918) 747-5009

Contents

Publisher's Note

The purpose of this book is to point the reader to God as our ultimate Healer. At the same time, however, it is important for the reader to understand that God uses many avenues to healing, including prayer, medicine, hospitals, surgery, nutrition, and exercise. The healing prayers of this book emphasize the importance of faith — a dynamic key in the healing process.

Faith draws us closer to God, and it also has a profound effect upon our mind, emotions, and body. The Scriptures impart faith to our hearts, and it is faith that unleashes the power of God's Word in our behalf. By praying the Scriptures we are put in touch with the heart of God — His will for us — and we are able to receive the blessings He has in store for us.

Therefore, in your search for healing, be sure to seek God at all times. Let His Word minister to your soul and spirit. Avail yourself of every avenue that God may use to effect healing in your life. Ask Him for wisdom with regard to the appropriate course to take. Sometimes God heals us without medical intervention, and at other times, He heals us through physicians, surgery, medicine, nutrition, exercise or a combination of means. Let Him guide you every step of the way.

This book is not meant to take the place of any medical advice you may have received. Rather, it is designed to go hand and hand with any avenue to healing you may have chosen. Always remember to keep looking to God as the One who ultimately heals, and to believe that He is at work in you and in your life. He loves you with an everlasting love.

This book is not intended to supply medical advice. In the event of any type of illness, do not neglect to consult your physician.

Introduction

We are so glad you have selected *Healing Prayers* to use in your search for healing and spiritual growth. This is a book of healing promises and healing prayers. There are over 100 topical prayers that are built directly from the Bible for you to use in expressing your faith to God.

These prayers are dynamic, personal, and inspiring, and they enable you to reach out for all God has in store for you — healing for your body, healing for your emotions, and healing for your mind.

You were created in the image of God who is a Trinity — Father, Son, and Holy Spirit. Like Him, you are a tripartite being — body, soul, and spirit. The teaching and the prayers contained in *Healing Prayers* are designed to help you to find wholeness for your body, soul, and spirit.

Our prayer for you, dear readers, is that like the Ephesians for whom the Apostle Paul prayed, you will experience all the fullness of God for your life: ". . .that He would grant you, according to the riches of His glory, to be strengthened with might through His Spirit in the inner man, that Christ may dwell in your hearts through faith; that you, being rooted and grounded in love, may be able to comprehend with all the saints what is the width and length and depth and height — to know the love of Christ which passes knowledge; that you may be filled with all the fullness of God. Now to Him who is able to do exceedingly abundantly above all that we ask or think, according to the power that works in us, to Him be glory in the church by Christ Jesus to all generations, forever and ever. Amen." (Eph. 3:16-21, NKJV).

We also hope you will take a moment to let us know how this book has ministered to you. We look forward to hearing how God has touched your life through *Healing Prayers*. May God bless you, keep you, and heal you.

Clift and Kathleen Richards
Victory House, Inc.
P.O. Box 700238
Tulsa, OK 74170

1

Healing Promises

The Bible assures us time and again that God wants His children to walk in health. That we can experience His healing power is affirmed throughout the Scriptures as the following promises of healing declare.

"If you diligently heed the voice of the Lord your God and do what is right in His sight, give ear to His commandments and keep all His statutes, I will put none of the diseases on you which I have brought on the Egyptians. For I am the Lord who heals you" (Exod. 15:26, NKJV).

"Bless the Lord, O my soul, and forget not all His benefits: Who forgives all your iniquities, Who heals all your diseases" (Ps. 103:2-3, NKJV).

"He sent His word and healed them, and delivered them from their destructions" (Ps. 107:20, NKJV).

"My son, give attention to my words; incline your ear to my sayings. Do not let them depart from your eyes; keep them in the midst of your heart; for they are life to those who find them, and health to all their flesh" (Prov. 4:20-22, NKJV).

"A merry heart does good, like medicine, but a broken spirit dries the bones" (Prov. 17:22, NKJV).

"But He [Jesus] was wounded for our transgressions, He was bruised for our iniquities; the chastisement for our peace was upon Him, and by His stripes we are healed" (Isa. 53:5, NKJV).

"Heal me, O Lord, and I shall be healed; save me, and I shall be saved, for You are my praise" (Jer. 17:14, NKJV).

"For I will restore health to you, and heal you of your wounds" (Jer. 30:17, NKJV).

"I will seek what was lost and bring back what was driven away, bind up the broken and strengthen what was sick" (Ezek. 34:16, NKJV).

"The centurion answered and said, 'Lord, I am not worthy that You should come under my roof. But only speak a word, and my servant will be healed'" (Matt. 8:8, NKJV).

"Be of good cheer, daughter; your faith has made you well" (Matt. 9:22, NKJV).

"Then Jesus went about all the cities and villages, teaching in their synagogues, preaching the gospel of the kingdom, and healing every sickness and every disease among the people" (Matt. 9:35, NKJV).

"And He said to her, 'Daughter, your faith has made you well. Go in peace, and be healed of your affliction'" (Mark 5:34, NKJV).

"And as many as touched Him were made well" (Mark 6:56, NKJV).

"He laid His hands on every one of them and healed them" (Luke 4:40, NKJV).

"And the whole multitude sought to touch Him, for power went out from Him and healed them all" (Luke 6:19, NKJV).

"Then Peter said, 'Silver and gold I do not have, but what I do have I give you: In the name of Jesus Christ of Nazareth, rise up and walk.' And he took him by the right hand and lifted him up, and immediately his feet and ankle bones received strength. So he, leaping up, stood and walked and entered the temple with them — walking, leaping, and praising God" (Acts 3:6-8, NKJV).

"Let it be known to you all, and to all the people of Israel, that by the name of Jesus Christ of Nazareth, whom you crucified, whom God raised from the dead, by Him this man stands here before you whole" (Acts 4:10, NKJV).

"Also a multitude gathered from the surrounding cities to Jerusalem, bringing sick people and those who were tormented by unclean spirits, and they were all healed" (Acts 5:16, NKJV).

"And Peter said to him, 'Aeneas, Jesus the Christ heals you. Arise and make your bed.' Then he arose immediately" (Acts 9:34, NKJV).

"And in Lystra a certain man without strength in his feet was sitting, a cripple from his mother's womb, who had never walked. This man heard Paul speaking. Paul, observing him intently and seeing that he had faith to be healed, said with a loud voice, 'Stand up straight on your feet!' And he leaped and walked" (Acts 14:8-10, NKJV).

"And the prayer of faith will save the sick, and the Lord will raise him up" (James 5:15, NKJV).

"Who Himself bore our sins in His own body on the tree, that we, having died to sins, might live for righteousness — by whose stripes you were healed" (1 Pet. 2:24, NKJV).

"Beloved, I pray that you may prosper in all things and be in health, just as your soul prospers" (3 John 2, NKJV).

"Jesus Christ is the same yesterday, today, and forever" (Heb. 13:8, NKJV).

2

The Promise of Healing

Faith — an Important Key to Healing

Review the healing promises we shared in chapter one. In the process of doing so, you will find your faith rising to receive God's promise of healing for your body, soul, and spirit. Did you notice how faith is such an integral part of the healing process? Time and time again the Scriptures show us that the promise of healing is connected to our faith — an important key to being healed.

Faith is imparted to us through the Holy Scriptures. Paul wrote, "So then faith comes by hearing, and hearing by the word of God" (Rom. 10:17, NKJV). It is so important for you to stay in the Word because the Word of God is: ". . .living and powerful, and sharper than any two-edged sword, piercing even to the division of soul and spirit, and of joints and marrow, and is a discerner of the thoughts and intents of the heart" (Heb. 4:12, NKJV).

The Psalmist tells us that God's Word is directly related to our healing. "He sent his word, and healed them, and delivered them from their destructions" (Ps. 107:20).

The Apostle John encourages us by saying, "And whatsoever we ask, we receive of him, because we keep his commandments, and do those things that are pleasing in his sight. And this is his commandment, That we should believe on the name of his Son Jesus Christ, and love one another, as he gave us commandment" (1 John 3:22-23). This passage points out that faith works by love in our lives. (See Gal. 5:6)

The statutes, principles, and command-ments of God are clearly delineated in His Word. The more you immerse yourself in the Word the more you will understand what God expects of you and how you may please Him in every area of your life. It's a wonder-ful process of spiritual growth and discovery.

The Bible says, "But without faith it is impossible to please Him, for he who comes to God must believe that He is, and that He is a rewarder of those who diligently seek Him" (Heb. 11:6, NKJV).

As your Rewarder, God wants you to walk in wholeness — body, soul, and spirit — in divine health. As your Father, He wants you to experience His healing power.

When we walk with the Lord
in the light of His Word,
What a glory He sheds on our way!
While we do His good will
He abides with us still,
And with all who will trust and obey.
Trust and obey, for there's no other way
To be happy in Jesus, but to trust and obey.
("When We Walk With the Lord" by
Daniel B. Towner, 1887)

God loves you!

Wholeness and Soundness

To heal, according to *Webster's New Collegiate Dictionary*, is "to make sound or whole, to restore to health, to cause an undesirable condition to be overcome, to mend, to patch up, to restore to original purity or integrity, to return to a sound state." These definitions show you that healing is a return to wholeness and soundness, two qualities that were stolen from you because of the disobedient acts that took place in the Garden of Eden.

As you know, Adam and Eve experienced perfect happiness and health prior to their choices to disobey God. God loved them, and they enjoyed wonderful fellowship with Him in the Garden — a paradise of beauty, wholeness, and joy. When they displeased God, however, through disobedience (stemming from a lack of faith), they lost their right to healing and health as well as happiness and peace.

Unfortunately, the results of the first couple's disobedience have been passed on to you. Therefore, you have become subject to the frailties of the flesh — sickness, disease, and death. These conditions, though, are not God's will for you. He wants His children to be blessed with good health, abundant life, and happiness. That's why He sent Jesus to be the sacrifice for your sins, and the Great Physician of your soul and body.

Jesus' death on the cross enables you to draw close to God, and His crucifixion has made it possible for you to find freedom from sin, illness, and spiritual death. The Apostle Peter wrote, "Who his own self bare our sins in his own body on the tree, that we, being dead to sins, should live unto righteousness: by whose stripes ye were healed" (1 Pet. 2:24). The stripes of Jesus brought forth blood, and it is the blood of Jesus that gives you the victory over sin, sickness, and death.

Jesus demonstrated His healing power over and over again as He walked among people. He is the Christ, the Anointed One, and God commissioned Him to ". . .preach the gospel to the poor. . .to heal the brokenhearted, to proclaim liberty to the captives and recovery of sight to the blind, to set at liberty those who are oppressed; to proclaim the acceptable year of the Lord" (Luke 4:18-19, NKJV).

That's exactly what Jesus did when He was on earth: "And Jesus went about all the cities and villages, teaching in their synagogues, and preaching the gospel of the kingdom, and healing *every* sickness and *every* disease among the people" (Matt. 9:35, italics ours).

Jesus is still ministering His healing power among us today, for He is ". . .the same yesterday, and today, and forever" (Heb. 13:8).

The Healing Ministry of Doctors

How greatly we respect the medical profession, which has come to our aid on so many different occasions. *Healing Prayers*, therefore, is not a book of medical advice. Please be careful to heed the recommendations of your physicians as you pray the prayers in this book.

God often uses doctors, specialists, and surgery to aid you in your quest for healing. In fact, one of the disciples of Jesus, Luke, was a physician, and many scholars believe that he practiced the medicine of his day while at the same time chronicling the healing ministry of his Master.

Healing Prayers is not meant to take the place of any medical advice you may have received. Rather, it is designed to go hand in hand with any avenue to healing you may have chosen. Always remember, however, to keep looking to God as the One who ultimately heals, and to believe that He is at work in every area of your life to effect the healing you need.

The Healing Ministry of Jesus Christ

Luke wrote the following words about Jesus, the Great Physician, "The power of the Lord was with him to heal" (Luke 5:17). This is an omnipotent power, without any limitations whatsoever. Paul prayed, "Now to Him who is able to do exceedingly abundantly above all that we ask or think, according to the power that works in us, to Him be glory in the church by Christ Jesus to all generations, forever and ever. Amen" (Eph. 3:20-21, NKJV).

God is able to do exceedingly abundantly above all that you ask or think (including healing), according to the power that is at work in you. What is this power that is at work in you? It is the Holy Spirit. He is the anointing that abides in every believer. (See 1 John 2:27.)

God promises that, "If the Spirit of Him who raised Jesus from the dead dwells in you, He who raised Christ from the dead will also give life to your mortal bodies through His Spirit who dwells in you" (Rom. 8:11, NKJV). In fact, the Bible promises you, "And my God shall supply all your need [including physical health and healing] according to His riches in glory by Christ Jesus" (Phil. 4:19, NKJV).

What wonderful promises these are to claim, and they are promises to you and for you, no matter what your need may be. The miraculous power of God is displayed for all to see in the Bible, and that dynamic power brought healing to the blind, the deaf, the diseased, the handicapped, lepers, epileptics, people with blood-related diseases, demoniacs, and ". . .every sickness and every disease among the people" (Matt. 9:35).

The healing ministry of Jesus Christ is so important, in fact, that one in every seven verses of the gospels deal with healing. Sometimes Jesus healed specific individuals and many times He healed entire groups of people at once.

Jesus Is Still a Healer

A minister friend of ours went to the hospital to visit with a church member who was in a coma. He wondered what he could possibly offer this woman who had been unconscious for over a week due to injuries she sustained in an automobile accident.

As he entered her room, a physician at her bedside looked at the pastor and said, "We're doing all we can for her. Let me encourage you to pray for her aloud, and read the Bible to her. The healing words of prayer and the Bible could reach her spirit."

The minister said, "You've given me my answer, doctor. When I was on my way to the hospital I wondered what I could possibly do for this lady in her present condition. Thank you for giving me the right answer."

So our friend did exactly that. First, he prayed for the parishioner's healing, then he began to read healing Scriptures aloud to her. He read one promise after another. The next day he returned and did the same thing. He did this for three days in succession. Finally, on the third day, as he was reading, he noticed the woman's eyelids begin to flutter, and he believed that the power of God's Word was bringing healing to her.

The next morning, as he was praying in his study, the phone rang. It was the previously comatose lady he had been visiting and praying for! In a weak voice, she said, "Pastor, thank you for ministering to me. Last night Jesus came into my room and healed me!"

The pastor's prayers and Bible reading had paved the way for Jesus to come and touch His daughter, bringing health and wholeness to her body.

There are countless other examples of Jesus' healing power in people's lives today. We heard of another lady who was suffering from a brain hemorrhage. After being rushed to the hospital she learned that emergency surgery to repair an aneurysm was required. The hospital chaplain prayed with her as she was being wheeled toward the operating room.

The aides rapidly pushed her gurney through the doors leading to the place of surgery. They stopped for a moment, and the woman with the hemorrhage noticed a little, old lady in a wheelchair with her Bible open on her lap. The lady began to read some healing promises aloud.

This ministered peace and comfort to the woman who had been in great pain, and she was surprised to discover that her pain became less intense. She smiled at the older woman as the orderlies pushed her through the doors into the operating room. God's healing power was already at work, and the lady's surgery was a tremendous success.

Notice how the power of prayer and the power of the Word combined to effect healing in the lives of these two women. Through these means, Jesus, the Great Physician, brought wholeness to them, and He restored their health. The promise of His healing power is available to you today as well.

"Jesus turned him about, and when he saw her, he said, 'Daughter, be of good comfort; thy faith hath made thee whole. And the woman was made whole from that hour" (Matt. 9:22).

The Healing Power of the Church

Jesus sent forth His disciples with spiritual authority: "He gave them power over unclean spirits, to cast them out, and to heal all kinds of sickness and all kinds of disease" (Matt. 10:1, NKJV). Power to heal all kinds of sickness and all kinds of disease was imparted to the disciples of Jesus Christ.

Jesus commanded them, "Whatever city you enter, and they receive you, eat such things as are set before you. And heal the sick there, and say to them, 'The kingdom of God has come near to you'" (Luke 10:8-9, NKJV). These faithful men fulfilled their commission as Mark clearly points out, "And they cast out many demons, and anointed with oil many who were sick, and healed them" (Mark 6:13, NKJV).

This gift of healing remains with the Church of Jesus Christ today. It is a gift that is conferred upon the Church by the Holy Spirit, as Paul points out, "But the manifestation of the Spirit is given to each one for the profit of all: for to one is given the word of wisdom through the Spirit, to another the word of knowledge through the same Spirit, to another faith by the same Spirit, to another gifts of healings by the same Spirit, to another the working of miracles, . . . But one and the same Spirit works all these things, distributing to each one individually as He wills" (1 Cor. 12:7-11, NKJV). These are the gifts of the Holy Spirit to the Body of Christ.

The healing power of Jesus Christ has been delegated to believers because we have been transferred into the Kingdom of God's beloved Son. (See Col. 1:13.) The demonstration of this mighty power filled people with awe when the apostles ministered healing to the sick, and this awesome power continues to astonish people today.

When Peter and John brought a healing miracle to the lame man who sat begging for alms at the Beautiful Gate of the Temple, the people who witnessed the miracle ". . .were filled with wonder and amazement at what had happened to him" (Acts 3:10, NKJV).

Peter responded to the people with these words: "Men of Israel, why do you marvel at this? Or why look so intently at us, as though by our own power or godliness we had made this man walk? The God of Abraham, Isaac, and Jacob, the God of our fathers, glorified His Servant Jesus, whom you delivered up and denied in the presence of Pilate, when he was determined to let Him go. But you denied the Holy One and the Just, and asked for a murderer to be granted to you, and killed the Prince of life, whom God raised from the dead, of which we are witnesses. And His name, through faith in His name, has made this man strong, whom you see and know. Yes, the faith which comes through Him has given him this perfect soundness in the presence of you all" (Acts 3:12-16, NKJV).

It was faith in the name of Jesus Christ that brought healing to the lame man, and faith in the name of Jesus still brings healing today.

Faith in the Name of Jesus

To pray in the name of Jesus is to pray in the power and authority of the Son of God. To minister in the name of Jesus is to minister in the same power and authority that Jesus demonstrated.

Jesus promises, "And whatsoever ye shall ask in my name, that will I do, that the Father may be glorified in the Son" (John 14:13). When we ask for healing in the name of Jesus we acknowledge His power to heal, and He promises to answer our prayer so that God will be glorified. "Whatsoever ye shall ask the Father in my name, he will give it you" (John 16:23).

Nothing is impossible with God. Jesus said, "All things are possible to him who believes" (Mark 9:23, NKJV). The power and authority inherent in the blessed name of Jesus are unleashed by faith. It truly is extraordinary power, and Jesus promises, "Most assuredly, I say to you, he who believes in Me, the works that I do he will do also; and greater works than these he will do, because I go to My Father" (John 14:12, NKJV).

Jesus healed all manner of sickness and disease, and He said that we will be able, through faith in His name, to experience His healing works today. The key, our Master tells us, is faith. "But without faith it is impossible to please Him, for he who comes to God must believe that He is, and that He is a rewarder of those who diligently seek Him" (Heb. 11:6, NKJV).

3

Prayer Promises

The promise of healing is effected through the prayer of faith that is rooted in the authority of Jesus Christ. James writes, "And the prayer of faith will save the sick, and the Lord will raise him up" (James 5:15, NKJV).

The following Scriptures are specific prayer promises from God's Word. When you incorporate these promises into your prayer life your faith will rise to enable you to appropriate healing and every other blessing that God has in store for you. As you experience God's healing in your life you will be able to help others who may need healing as well.

"The Lord is my rock and my fortress and my deliverer; the God of my strength, in whom I will trust; my shield and the horn of my salvation, my stronghold and my refuge; my Savior, You save me from violence. I will call upon the Lord, who is worthy to be praised; so shall I be saved from my enemies" (2 Sam. 22:2-4, NKJV).

"In my distress I called upon the Lord, and cried out to my God; He heard my voice from His temple, and my cry entered His ears" (2 Sam. 22:7, NKJV).

"Return and tell Hezekiah the leader of My people, 'Thus says the Lord, the God of David your father: 'I have heard your prayer, I have seen your tears; surely I will heal you" (2 Kings 20:5, NKJV).

"He hears the cry of the afflicted" (Job 34:28, NKJV).

"But know that the Lord has set apart for Himself him who is godly; the Lord will hear when I call to Him" (Ps. 4:3, NKJV).

"He does not forget the cry of the humble" (Ps. 9:12, NKJV).

"Blessed be the Lord, because He has heard the voice of my supplications!" (Ps. 28:6, NKJV).

"I sought the Lord, and He heard me, and delivered me from all my fears" (Ps. 34:4, NKJV).

"This poor man cried out, and the Lord heard him, and saved him out of all his troubles" (Ps. 34:6, NKJV).

"Offer to God thanksgiving, and pay your vows to the Most High. Call upon Me in the day of trouble; I will deliver you, and you shall glorify Me" (Ps. 50:14-15, NKJV).

"Because he has set his love upon Me, therefore I will deliver him; I will set him on high, because he has known My name. He shall call upon Me, and I will answer him; I will be with him in trouble; I will deliver him and honor him. With long life I will satisfy him, and show him My salvation" (Ps. 91:14-16, NKJV).

"In my distress I cried to the Lord, and He heard me" (Ps. 120:1, NKJV).

"The Lord is near to all who call upon Him, to all who call upon Him in truth. He will fulfill the desire of those who fear Him; He also will hear their cry and save them" (Ps. 145:18-19, NKJV).

"The Lord is far from the wicked, but He hears the prayer of the righteous" (Prov. 15:29, NKJV).

"Then you will call upon Me and go and pray to Me, and I will listen to you. And you will seek Me and find Me, when you search for Me with all your heart. I will be found by you, says the Lord, and I will bring you back from your captivity" (Jer. 29:12-14, NKJV).

"Call to Me, and I will answer you, and show you great and mighty things, which you do not know" (Jer. 33:3, NKJV).

"And it shall come to pass that whoever calls on the name of the Lord shall be saved" (Joel 2:32, NKJV).

"They will call on My name, and I will answer them. I will say, 'This is My people'; and each one will say, 'The Lord is my God.'" (Zech. 13:9, NKJV).

"Your Father knows the things you have need of before you ask Him" (Matt. 6:8, NKJV).

"Ask, and it will be given to you; seek, and you will find; knock, and it will be opened to you. For everyone who asks receives, and he who seeks finds, and to him who knocks it will be opened" (Matt. 7:7-8, NKJV).

"If you then, being evil, know how to give good gifts to your children, how much more will your Father who is in heaven give good things to those who ask Him!" (Matt. 7:11, NKJV).

"Again I say to you that if two of you agree on earth concerning anything that they ask, it will be done for them by My Father in heaven. For where two or three are gathered together in My name, I am there in the midst of them" (Matt. 18:19-20, NKJV).

"And whatever things you ask in prayer, believing, you will receive" (Matt. 21:22, NKJV).

"Have faith in God. For assuredly, I say to you, whoever says to this mountain, 'Be removed and be cast into the sea,' and does not doubt in his heart, but believes that those things he says will be done, he will have whatever he says. Therefore I say to you, whatever things you ask when you pray, believe that you receive them, and you will have them" (Mark 11:22-24, NKJV).

"And whatever you ask in My name, that I will do, that the Father may be glorified in the Son. If you ask anything in My name, I will do it" (John 14:13-14, NKJV).

"If you abide in Me, and My words abide in you, you will ask what you desire, and it shall be done for you" (John 15:7, NKJV).

"Most assuredly, I say to you, whatever you ask the Father in My name He will give you" (John 16:23, NKJV).

"Until now you have asked nothing in My name. Ask, and you will receive, that your joy may be full" (John 16:24, NKJV).

"For there is no distinction between Jew and Greek, for the same Lord over all is rich to all who call upon Him" (Rom. 10:12, NKJV).

"Now to Him who is able to do exceedingly abundantly above all that we ask or think, according to the power that works in us, to Him be glory in the church by Christ Jesus to all generations, forever and ever. Amen" (Eph. 3:20-21, NKJV).

"Be anxious for nothing, but in everything by prayer and supplication, with thanksgiving, let your requests be made known to God; and

the peace of God, which surpasses all understanding, will guard your hearts and minds
through Christ Jesus" (Phil. 4:6-7, NKJV).

"Rejoice always, pray without ceasing, in
everything give thanks; for this is the will of God
in Christ Jesus for you" (1 Thess. 5:16-18, NKJV).

"He who calls you is faithful, who also
will do it" (1 Thess. 5:24, NKJV).

"Therefore I exhort first of all that supplications, prayers, intercessions, and giving of
thanks be made for all men, for kings and all
who are in authority, that we may lead a quiet
and peaceable life in all godliness and
reverence. For this is good and acceptable in the
sight of God our Savior" (1 Tim. 2:1-3, NKJV).

"I desire therefore that the men pray
everywhere, lifting up holy hands, without
wrath and doubting" (1 Tim. 2:8, NKJV).

"Let us therefore come boldly to the
throne of grace, that we may obtain mercy
and find grace to help in time of need" (Heb.
4:16, NKJV).

"But without faith it is impossible to please
Him, for he who comes to God must believe
that He is, and that He is a rewarder of those
who diligently seek Him" (Heb. 11:6, NKJV).

"If any of you lacks wisdom, let him ask of
God, who gives to all liberally and without

reproach, and it will be given to him. But let him ask in faith, with no doubting, for he who doubts is like a wave of the sea driven and tossed by the wind. For let not that man suppose that he will receive anything from the Lord" (James 1:5-7, NKJV).

"You do not have because you do not ask" (James 4:2, NKJV).

"And the prayer of faith will save the sick, and the Lord will raise him up" (James 5:15, NKJV).

"The effective, fervent prayer of a righteous man avails much" (James 5:16, NKJV).

"For the eyes of the Lord are on the righteous, and His ears are open to their prayers; but the face of the Lord is against those who do evil" (1 Pet. 3:12, NKJV).

"And whatever we ask we receive from Him, because we keep His commandments and do those things that are pleasing in His sight" (1 John 3:22, NKJV).

"Now this is the confidence that we have in Him, that if we ask anything according to His will, He hears us. And if we know that He hears us, whatever we ask, we know that we have the petitions that we have asked of Him" (1 John 5:14-15, NKJV).

"And the smoke of the incense, with the prayers of the saints, ascended before God from the angel's hand" (Rev. 8:4, NKJV).

4

The Promise of Prayer

Prayer — an Avenue to Healing

Take a moment now to review the prayer promises that are cited in chapter 3. Did you notice how your faith has risen as a result of reading those dynamic promises? In addition to the power of God's Word, the power of faith, and the power of Jesus' name, you are privileged to be able to draw upon the power of prayer in order to find healing for your life. God will hear and answer your prayer for healing.

Notice what happens when you express your faith to God through prayer:

1. You will be saved from violence and all enemies. (See 2 Sam. 22:3-4.)

2. You will be healed. (See 2 Kings 20:5.)

3. You will be delivered from all your fears. (See Ps. 34:4.)

4. You will not be ashamed. (See Ps. 34:5.)

5. You will be saved out of all your troubles. (See Ps. 34:6.)

6. You will be delivered. (See Ps. 50:14-15.)

7. You will be honored. (See Ps. 91:15.)

8. You will be satisfied. (See Ps. 91:16.)

9. You will see great and mighty things which you do not presently know. (See Jer. 33:3.)

10. You will receive what you requested. (See Matt. 21:22.)

11. Your joy will be full. (See John 16:24.)

12. You will know God's peace. (See Phil. 4:6-7.)

13. You will lead a quiet and peaceable life in all godliness and honesty. (See 1 Tim. 2:1-3.)

14. You will obtain mercy and find grace to help you. (See Heb. 4:16.)

15. You will have wisdom. (See James 1:5.)

16. You will have the petitions you present to God. (See 1 John 5:15.)

17. Your prayers will ascend before God in heaven. (See Rev. 8:4.)

All of these blessings will be yours when you pray in faith, nothing wavering, and these prayer promises assure you of healing and wholeness for your body, soul, and spirit as well as innumerable other blessings.

Praying God's Word

As you will soon discover, the following sections of this book contain topical prayers that come directly from the Word of God. These Bible prayers are for you to use in seeking healing for your life. By praying the Scriptures you can be certain that you are praying God's will for your life, because you know that His will is revealed in the Bible.

It is important to pray Bible promises for several reasons:

1. They are powerful.
2. They build our faith.
3. They represent the will of God to us.
4. They assure us that God is willing and able to heal us.
5. They bring results.
6. They please God.
7. They are truth.
8. They lead us in the paths of righteousness.

John wrote, "And this is the confidence that we have in him, that, if we ask anything according to his will, he heareth us. And if we know that he hear us, whatsoever we ask, we know that we have the petitions that we desired of him" (1 John 5:14-15).

Great confidence will come to you as you pray the Bible — a confidence that comes from knowing that God hears you when you pray and that He will grant your petitions. Jesus said, "If ye abide in me, and my words abide in you, ye shall ask what ye will, and it shall be done unto you" (John 15:7).

As you pray these Word-based prayers, you will gain new insights into God's thoughts and desires for you. In fact, He promises, "I will visit you and perform My good word toward you, and cause you to return to this place. For I know the thoughts that I think toward you, says the Lord, thoughts of peace and not of evil, to give you a future and a hope. Then you will call upon Me and go and pray to Me, and I will listen to you, and you will seek Me and find Me, . . .I will be found by you, says the Lord" (Jer. 29:10-14, NKJV).

Isn't it wonderful to know that God thinks thoughts of peace toward you, and He wants to give you a future and a hope? These are healing thoughts, and they come right from the heart of God. Use this verse as the spring-board for diving into the power and glory of *Healing Prayers*.

It may be trite, but it is nonetheless true, that prayer changes things. In fact, many circumstances cannot be changed except through the power of prayer. Such is often the case with healing.

As we meditate on the truths and promises of the Bible, our attitudes, thoughts, and behaviors change. This has a dramatic impact on our bodies and minds. We are cleansed from within and we are empowered to do battle against illness in whatever form it presents itself. These Bible truths are life to us and health to all our flesh. (See Prov. 4: 20-22.)

The principles of prayer that we outline in *Healing Prayers* are God's, not ours. As you incorporate them into your own prayer life, your prayers will become fruitful, powerful, and prosperous, and you will experience the healing power of God at work in your life.

God Is Your Healer, and He Is Your Health

The Psalmist writes, "Why art thou cast down, O my soul? And why art thou disquieted within me? Hope in God: for I shall yet praise him, who is the health of my countenance, and my God" (Ps. 43:5).

Health is a law of God's kingdom, and He is the true Fountain of life, health, and happiness. Healing flows from His hands. He promises, "I will restore health to you, and your wounds I will heal" (Jer. 30:17, RSV).

God is the author of life, and He wants you to experience life to the fullest.

When Adam and Eve sinned in the Garden, Satan gained a certain degree of legal rights and access in the earth, allowing him to afflict mankind. This is part of the reason why the Apostle Paul calls Satan, "the god of this world." Oppression from the devil may result in illness. Acts 10:38 tells us that Jesus went about doing good and healing all that were oppressed of the devil.

In the thirteenth chapter of the Gospel of Luke the story is told of a woman who was healed by Jesus. The woman had been bent over for eighteen years under the oppression of a spirit of infirmity. She could not even straighten herself up. Jesus healed the woman, and when the ruler of the synagogue protested because Jesus had healed on the Sabbath, Jesus responded by saying, "So ought not this woman, being a daughter of Abraham, whom Satan has bound . . .for eighteen years be loosed from this bond on the Sabbath?" (Luke 13:10-16, NKJV.)

Jesus said, "The thief [Satan] does not come except to steal, and to kill, and to destroy. I have come that they may have life, and that they may have it more abundantly" (John 10:10, NKJV).

The biblical examples show us that at least some sickness is the direct result of oppression from Satan. The good news is that Jesus has already defeated Satan. Not only that, Jesus has given all believers authority over Satan and his minions in order to enforce the victory that He won for us.

Jesus told his disciples, "Behold, I give you the authority to trample on serpents and scorpions, and over all the power of the enemy, and nothing shall by any means hurt you" (Luke 10:19, NKJV).

At the annual Christian Booksellers Convention we frequently have the opportunity to pray with people who are feeling ill, tired, frightened, or exhausted. So many of the folks we pray for come back to us in subsequent years to tell us how our prayers have ministered to them. Such reports are always very encouraging and cause us to praise God for His goodness.

One bookseller, for example, came to our booth with an excruciating migraine headache. It caused her to feel quite disoriented and nauseated. After our brief prayer, she began to cry. She said, "Thank you so much for praying for me. The pain is completely gone!"

Each year she returns to our booth to tell us what that experience meant to her. It is such a joy to be able to minister God's healing grace to other believers.

The Grace of God

Did you ever notice how Paul opens many of his epistles with a prayer for the recipients? In most of those prayers he asks for God's grace to be imparted to the believers. For example, soon after he opens his first epistle to the Corinthians, he prays, "Grace to you and peace from God our Father and the Lord Jesus Christ" (1 Cor. 1:3, NKJV).

Grace, as you know, is something we receive from God without earning it or deserving it. It is a gift. The word "grace" appears literally scores of times throughout the New Testament. To receive God's grace is to receive His favor and the accompanying ability or empowerment to accomplish God's plans and desires. You began your walk of experiencing God's favor when you were saved. "For by grace you have been saved through faith, and that not of yourselves; it is the gift of God, not of works, lest anyone should boast" (Eph. 2:8-9, NKJV). This is God's saving grace, and it is effected in your life through faith.

By God's grace we heard the Word preached. By God's grace faith arose in our hearts to believe the message of salvation through Christ. By God's grace we were empowered to believe and receive redemption from sin and have eternal life. The Apostle Paul said, "For I am not ashamed of the gospel of Christ, for it is the power of God to salvation for everyone who believes" (Rom. 1:16, NKJV). God's grace and God's power go hand in hand to accomplish God's plan.

This is true with regard to God's healing grace as well. In the same way that you began your Christian life through prayer and faith, asking God to forgive you and believing that

He raised Christ from the dead (See Rom. 10:8-9.), you experience God's healing love, power, and grace through prayer and belief. God's grace has brought you the faith, and that faith has empowered you to believe and receive God's healing power.

Notice how Isaiah focuses on grace as he proclaims God's goodness in his life: "I will mention the lovingkindnesses of the Lord and the praises of the Lord, according to all that the Lord has bestowed on us, and the great goodness toward the house of Israel, which He has bestowed on them according to His mercies, according to the multitude of His lovingkindnesses" (Isa. 63:7, NKJV).

There are over 3,000 promises in the Bible, and each one is a promise of God's grace and love for you. "For all the promises of God in Him are Yes, and in Him Amen, to the glory of God through us" (2 Cor. 1:20, NKJV).

As we pray the promises of God in order to seek His healing grace, we can hear these words echoing in our hearts, "I, the Lord, have spoken, and will do it" (Ezek. 22:14, NKJV).

Dear believer, God wants you to be well. He promises health and healing to you. His grace is sufficient for you. Therefore, think health and pray health. Praise God for His healing power. Believe His Word. Receive all that He has for you.

He gave you life, and He sustains your life. He is life itself. He is health. He is goodness.

Hear the Word of God. Focus on God's promises. Give life to His promises as you speak them forth. Listen to God's words instead of the devil's lies, and remember that the worst liars in the world are your own fears. Recall these words of George Macdonald: "A perfect faith would lift us absolutely above fear."

Faith is active, and faith-filled prayer releases God's power in your life. As you pray the *Healing Prayers* that follow, agree with the Word of God and surrender to His loving grace. Remember that God can do anything but fail. Don't ever give yourself the benefit of the doubt, because doubt has no benefits!

Jesus said, "All things are possible to him who believes" (Mark 9:23, NKJV). God will not fail you. Oswald Chambers wrote, "Our capacity in spiritual matters is measured by the promises of God." Those promises are for you. God gives us His promises so that we can receive His healing by faith, and real faith never goes home with an empty basket.

"For the Lord God is a sun and shield: the Lord will give grace and glory: no good thing will he withhold from them that walk uprightly" (Ps. 84:11).

"Let us therefore come boldly unto the throne of grace, that we may obtain mercy, and find grace to help in time of need" (Heb. 4:16).

God's

Greatest

Healing

Miracle

The Good News of Jesus Christ is that God has sent His only begotten Son to save us from the dominion of sin, evil, and death. Jesus said, "For God so loved the world that He gave His only begotten Son, that whoever believes in Him should not perish but have everlasting life. . . .He who believes in Him is not condemned; but he who does not believe is condemned already, because he has not believed in the name of the only begotten Son of God" (John 3:16-18, NKJV).

The name of the only begotten Son of God is Jesus. God sent Jesus to be a sacrifice for your sins. (See 1 John 2:1-2.) That's why Jesus died on the cross — to save you from the condemnation of sin, which Paul tells us is death. He writes, "For the wages of sin is death, but the gift of God is eternal life in Christ Jesus our Lord" (Rom. 6:23, NKJV).

The fact is that all of us have sinned and fallen short of the glory of God. (See Rom. 3:23.) This is why you need Jesus as your Savior, and in order to experience the wonderful miracle of salvation, you must accept and receive Jesus Christ as your personal Savior by faith.

Paul writes, "If you confess with your mouth the Lord Jesus and believe in your heart that God has raised Him from the dead, you will be saved. For with the heart one believes unto righteousness, and with the mouth confession is made unto salvation" (Rom. 10:9-10, NKJV).

Therefore, in order to avail yourself of the greatest healing miracle of all, you must believe in Jesus Christ as your Savior and Lord. As you pray the following scriptural prayer, open your heart, receive Him, and confess Him as your personal Savior and Lord.

Jesus loves you, and He wants you to become a child of God. In fact, this is His personal invitation to you, "But as many as received Him, to them gave He the right to become children of God, to those who believe on His name; who were born, not of blood, nor of the will of man, but of God" (John 1:12, NKJV).

Dear reader, when you pray the following prayer of salvation with faith in your heart, you will be born again, old things will pass away, and you will become a new creation in Christ Jesus. (See 2 Cor. 5:17.) This miraculous rebirth will make you a member of the family of God forever and you will receive eternal life. God loves you far more than you can possibly imagine, and He eagerly waits for you to pray the prayer of salvation, which is printed on the following page. It's exciting to know you are on the verge of receiving the greatest healing miracle of all — salvation!

1

Salvation — God's Greatest Miracle

A Prayer for You to Pray if You
Do Not Know Jesus as Your Savior

Healing Promise: *"For God so loved the world that He gave His only begotten Son, that whoever believes in Him should not perish but have everlasting life"* (John 3:16, NKJV).

Healing Prayer: Heavenly Father, thank you for sending your only begotten Son to die for me.[1] I believe in Jesus Christ,[2] and I believe you have raised Him from the dead.[3] Thank you, Father, for your wonderful promise of eternal life through Him.[4]

As I ponder your wonderful love for me,[5] I confess my sins to you in full repentance, realizing that you are forgiving me and cleansing me from all unrighteousness.[6] Thank you, Father.

Thank you for commending your love to me, in that while I was yet a sinner, Christ died for me.[7] Even though I now understand that the wages of sin are death, I also realize that your gift of grace to me is eternal life.[8]

Thank you for your grace at work in my life, dear Father, for it is through your grace that I know you are saving me, healing me, and making me whole.[9] I now realize that I can't make myself perfect or good, but that I am totally dependent on you for salvation.[10]

How I thank you for sending Jesus Christ into the world to save sinners.[11] I confess Him with my mouth, and I believe in my heart that you have raised Him from the dead,[12] paving the way for me to experience everlasting life.[13] Thank you, Father.

I rejoice in you, O Lord God, because I now know you have saved me. It is so wonderful to realize that, because I am now a new creation in Christ, the old things have passed away and you have made all things new.[14] Hallelujah! I've been born again through the incorruptible seed of your mighty Word, which lives and abides forever.[15]

Thank you, O God my Savior, for saving me and setting me free from the degradation of sin and eternal damnation. In Jesus' name I pray, Amen.[16]

References: (1) John 3:16; (2) Titus 3:4-6; (3) Romans 10:9; (4) John 3:16-17; (5) Romans 5:5; (6) 1 John 1:9; (7) Romans 5:8; (8) Romans 6:23; (9) Ephesians 2:8-9; (10) Ephesians 2:9; (11) Luke 19:10; (12) Romans 10:9; (13) John 3:16; (14) 2 Corinthians 5:17; (15) 1 Peter 1:23; (16) John 15:16.

Healing

For

Your

Body

Healing of the body is promised in both testaments of the holy Scriptures. The patriarchs and prophets of ancient times certainly regarded God as their Healer. Jesus became known as the Great Physician because He spent a major part of His ministry on earth healing people's bodies.

In fact, God anointed His Son, Jesus, to ". . .preach the gospel to the poor; . . .to heal the brokenhearted, to proclaim liberty to the captives and recovery of sight to the blind, to set at liberty those who are oppressed; to proclaim the acceptable year of the Lord" (Luke 4:18-19, NKJV).

He is still the same. The Bible says, "Jesus Christ is the same yesterday, today, and forever" (Heb. 13:8, NKJV). This clearly means that Jesus is still the Great Physician of our souls and bodies. What's more, He wants to heal His children. The prayers in this section of *Healing Prayers* are developed in such a way as to help you reach out for healing of diseases, illnesses, injuries, and other physical ailments. God wants you to walk in healing and health, and these prayers will help you appropriate divine health for your own life.

When Jesus walked among people on earth He ". . .laid his hands on every one of them, and healed them." As you pray these

Healing Prayers, reach out for His healing touch and experience His dynamic blessing in your life.

James wrote, "Is anyone among you suffering? Let him pray. Is anyone cheerful? Let him sing psalms. Is anyone among you sick? Let him call for the elders of the church, and let them pray over him, anointing him with oil in the name of the Lord. And the prayer of faith will save the sick, and the Lord will raise him up. . . .The effective, fervent prayer of a righteous man avails much" (James 5:13-16, NKJV).

2

A Prayer for Healing

A Healing Prayer to Use for Any Healing Need

Healing Promise: *"He sent his word, and healed them"* (Ps. 107:20).

Healing Prayer: Heavenly Father, I thank you for all the promises of your Word, which proclaim healing to those who are sick. Your Word is truth[1] and it is forever settled in heaven.[2] You tell me in your Word that you have provided healing for me through the stripes of Jesus Christ my Lord.[3] I believe your hands will make me whole[4] because this is the promise of your Word.

Mighty God, I take great joy from your promise that though the afflictions of the righteous may be many, you will deliver me and all your children out of them all.[5] Thank you, God, my Healer.[6]

You are always faithful, Father.[7] You fulfill all your promises and you do not lie.[8] Therefore, I ask you to remove all sickness from my body now as I pray.

Heal me of this sickness, O Lord God, and I know I will be healed.[9] Thank you for strengthening me.[10] You are the Lord God who is healing me.[11] As I reach out to touch the hem of the garment of the Great Physician, Jesus Christ,[12] I believe that I am receiving healing for this sickness[13] and I believe that you, Father God, are making me whole.

I rejoice in your promise that you will heal me of all my diseases.[14] Therefore, I bless you with all my soul, and all that is within me blesses your holy name, Father.[15]

With your help, I will endeavor to keep my heart merry each day, because I know that a merry heart does me good like a medicine.[16] Thank you, Father. I will endeavor to walk in the joy you impart to me, because I know your joy truly is my strength.[17] You fill me with all joy and peace as I believe your Word, and I abound in hope by the power of the Holy Spirit.[18]

Deliver me from all fear, thoughts, and imaginations the devil would bring to torment me.[19] Through faith in your Word, I now bring every thought, and all imaginations and rea-sonings into captivity to the obedience of Christ.[20] In the authority of the matchless name of Jesus Christ, I confront the devil, the enemy of my soul, and all related fears he attempts to assail me with, and I command him to stop his efforts against me now.[21]

This sickness has a name, Father, and your Word says that every name must bow its knee at the mere mention of the name of Jesus.[22]

Therefore, Father, in the name of Jesus,[23] through faith in that name,[24] and through the merits of the precious blood of Jesus Christ;[25] I now command this illness of _____ in my body to bow its knee, and to leave my body forever.[26] I ask you, Father, to watch over these words of faith and bring them to pass by your great power.[27]

Your Word imparts faith for healing to my heart.[28] I receive your Word, your strength, and I receive your healing now as I pray. I know that through Jesus I have been made whole.[29] Thank you, Father.

You have enabled me to have the faith I need to be healed.[30] I believe your healing power is working in me now. My prayer is a prayer of faith based upon your Word and the faith that you have imparted to me by your grace, and I know you are healing me and raising me up through your great power.[31] It is with joy that I receive healing, strength, and health from you now, Father. In Jesus' wonderful name I pray, Amen.[32] Thank you, Father.

References: *(1) John 17:17; (2) Psalms 119:89; (3) Isaiah 53:5; (4) Job 5:18; (5) Psalms 34:19; (6) Exodus 15:26; (7) Hebrews 10:23; (8) Titus 1:2; (9) Jeremiah 17:14; (10) Psalms 28:7; (11) Exodus 15:26; (12) Matthew 9:21; (13) Mark 11:24; (14) Psalms 103:3; (15) Psalms 103:1; (16) Proverbs 17:22; (17) Nehemiah 8:10; (18) Romans 15:13;*

(19) Joel 2:32; (20) 2 Corinthians 10:5; (21) James 4:7; (22) Philippians 2:10; (23) John 14:13; (24) Acts 3:16; (25) Revelation 12:11; (26) Mark 11:23; (27) Jeremiah 1:12; (28) Romans 10:17; (29) Acts 9:34; (30) Acts 14:9; (31) James 5:15; (32) John 16:23-24.

3

Addictions

A Healing Prayer to Use in
Overcoming Physical Addictions

Healing Promise: *"Stand fast therefore in the liberty by which Christ has made us free, and do not be entangled again with a yoke of bondage"* (Gal. 5:1, NKJV).

Healing Prayer: Dear Lord God, I've struggled with my addiction(s) to _____ for far too long. I need your help. Turn unto me and have mercy upon me, for I am desolate and afflicted.[1] I truly desire to commit all my works to you, Father, so my thoughts will be established in such a way that, with your help and through your grace, I will be able to conquer this addiction completely.[2]

I know you will help me, Lord God. Thank you for loving me. Therefore, I will not be confused or confounded in any way. I will set my face like a flint, and in so doing, I know I shall not be ashamed any longer.[3] Thank you for giving me a spirit of power, and of love, and of a sound mind.[4] I claim this promise now as I pray, and I thank you for delivering me from my addiction.[5]

Thank you for your faithfulness to me, Father. I express my faith to you that you are holding my hand, establishing me now, helping me, and keeping me from all evil, including my addiction(s).[6] Thank you, mighty God. With your help, from this day forth, I will stand fast in the liberty you've imparted to me so that I will never again be entangled with that yoke of bondage that has held me back for so long.[7] Thank you for setting me free, for whom the Son makes free is free indeed.[8]

Impart the mind of Christ to me, dear God, so that I will think as He does and live as He wants me to live.[9] With His help, I will bring all of my thoughts into captivity to the obedience of Christ.[10] In the name of Jesus, therefore, I resist the evil one — Satan — and I command him to depart from me.[11]

The curse of addiction in my life will not stand. I will rebuke the devil and his cohorts every time they try to tempt me.[12] Fill me afresh and continuously every day with the Holy Spirit, Father,[13] so that I will be able always to walk in the Spirit and thereby not fulfill the lusts of my flesh.[14] How I thank you that the indwelling Holy Spirit will guide me at all times.[15] In Jesus' name I pray, Amen.[16]

References: (1) Psalms 25:16; (2) Proverbs 16:3; (3) Isaiah 50:7; (4) 2 Timothy 1:7; (5) Psalms 31:15; (6) Isaiah 41:13;

(7) Galatians 5:1; (8) John 8:36; (9) 1 Corinthians 2:16; (10) 2 Corinthians 10:5; (11) James 4:7; (12) Jude 9; (13) Ephesians 5:18; (14) Galatians 5:16; (15) John 16:13; (16) John 15:16.

4

AIDS

A Healing Prayer to Use if
You Have AIDS/ HIV

Healing Promise: *"Bless the Lord, O my soul, and forget not all His benefits: who forgives all your iniquities, who heals all your diseases, who redeems your life from destruction, who crowns you with lovingkindness and tender mercies"* (Ps. 103:1-4, NKJV).

Healing Prayer: Heavenly Father, thank you for all the promises of your Word. They assure me that you have the power to heal me and you always want the best for me. Thank you, Father. Because I know these are truths of your Word, I come to you now, asking you to heal me of AIDS. I recognize this hideous disease as the enemy's curse in my life, and I stand against him in the name of Jesus Christ, rebuking him with the power you've imparted to me.[1] Thank you for the power of your great love in my life, Father.

How I thank you that you have forgiven me of all my iniquities, that in Christ you have already redeemed my life from destruction, and you have crowned me with your lovingkindness and your tender mercies. Your desire is to satisfy my mouth with the good things your grace has already provided for me in Christ, so that my youth will be renewed like the eagle's.[2] Praise you, Father.

I know and I believe that you will not allow me to want for any good thing in my life, Father.[3] Indeed, you have promised to supply all my needs according to your riches in glory through Christ Jesus.[4] You are my Shepherd, Lord God, and because this is true I know you will take care of all my needs, including my need for healing.[5] Thank you, Father.

I ask, also, that you would lead researchers to a cure for AIDS. Pour out your wisdom upon them and let them witness your great mercy and power. I will never forget your precepts, dear God, for through them I know you are quickening me.[6] Your powerful, living Word is sharper than any two-edged sword, and I am experiencing its power at work in me.[7] Thank you, God.

Others have tried to discourage me by saying that there is no hope for someone who has AIDS; but, Father, I believe the truthful promises of your Word, and they loudly proclaim to me that you are able to do exceeding abundantly beyond all that I could ever ask or think, according to the power that is at work in me by your Holy Spirit.[8]

I will meditate in your healing Word day and night so that my faith may increase and be strong, for I know that faith comes by hearing your Word.[9] Praise your mighty name, dear God, for you are the One who is healing me.[10]

Fill me with the Holy Spirit, Father.[11] I pray that I will experience His quickening, healing, and life-giving power in my body.[12] Help me to walk always in the Holy Spirit so that I will never fulfill the lusts of my flesh.[13] Thank you for healing me and making me whole. In Jesus' name I pray, Amen.[14]

References: (1) Jude 9; (2) Psalms 103:1-4; (3) Psalms 34:10; (4) Philippians 4:19; (5) Psalms 23:1; (6) Psalms 119:93; (7) Hebrews 4:12; (8) Ephesians 3:20; (9) Romans 10:17; (10) Exodus 15:26; (11) Ephesians 5:18; (12) Romans 8:11; (13) Galatians 5:16; (14) John 16:23.

5

Allergies

*A Healing Prayer to Use When
You Suffer From Allergies*

Healing Promise: *"Surely He has borne our griefs and carried our sorrows; yet we esteemed Him stricken, smitten by God, and afflicted. But He was wounded for our transgressions, He was bruised for our iniquities; the chastisement for our peace was upon Him, and by His stripes we are healed"* (Isa. 53:4-5, NKJV).

Healing Prayer: Dear God, allergies have often afflicted me and made my life miserable. I know this is not your will for me. Heal me, Father. Thank you for your great love in my life.

Father God, thank you for sending Jesus to die for me. How grateful I am for His willingness to take my sin and sickness upon Him. I accept the fact that I am being healed of my allergies by His stripes.[1] O Lord my God, I cry unto you, and you are healing me.[2] Thank you, Almighty God, my Father.

I will attend to your words, Lord God, and incline my ear to all your sayings. I will be careful not to let them depart from my eyes, and I will keep them in the midst of my heart, because I know that they are life and health to me.[3] Praise you for your Word, dear God.

All of my hope is in you, Father. I will yet praise you, because I know you are the health of my countenance and my God.[4] Therefore, I completely trust you to heal me of all allergies. Thank you for giving me life, breath, and all things.[5]

Heal me, O Lord God, and I know I shall be completely healed, because this is the promise of your Word.[6] Send your Word and heal me, and deliver me from all destructions and illnesses.[7] Now, as I pray, I claim your promise that you will heal me of all diseases, which includes these allergies.[8]

Thank you for the wonderful desire you've expressed for me, that I would prosper and be in health even as my soul prospers.[9] I believe and claim this promise from your Word, dear God, and I thank you for total healing from allergies.

Thank you for showing me that allergies, like all illnesses, are not your will for me. In fact, they are a curse from the enemy. Therefore, I take my stand against him. I resist the devil in the name of Jesus Christ, and he must flee from me according to your Word, Father.[10]

I proclaim that Jesus is my Lord and he came to give me abundant life.[11] Now that you've healed me of these allergies, Father, I can enjoy the abundance Jesus has imparted to me, and I can serve you more fully. Hallelujah! In Jesus' name I pray, Amen.[12]

References: (1) Isaiah 53:4-5; (2) Psalms 30:2; (3) Proverbs 4:20-22; (4) Psalms 42:11; (5) Acts 17:25; (6) Jeremiah 17:14; (7) Psalms 107:20; (8) Psalms 103:3; (9) 3 John 2; (10) James 4:7; (11) John 10:10; (12) John 15:16.

6

Alzheimer's Disease

*A Healing Prayer to Use When You Are
Diagnosed With Alzheimer's Disease*

Healing Promise: *"Behold, I will bring it health and
healing; I will heal them and reveal to them the abundance
of peace and truth"* (Jer. 33:6, NKJV).

Healing Prayer: Dear God, the diagnosis of
Alzheimer's disease has greatly disturbed me
and the members of my family. Therefore, I
come to you now in order to claim your
wonderful promise to bring health and
healing to me. Father, heal me and reveal to
me and my family the abundance of your
truth and peace.[1] I believe that your eyes are
over me and your ears are open to my
prayers.[2] Thank you for this promise from
your Word.

As I rest in you, Lord God, and wait
patiently for you, I will not fret, because I
know you are at work in my life.[3] You are my
refuge in times of trouble.[4] Praise your mighty
name. As I commit my works to you, I know
you will establish my thoughts.[5] Father, I
know you will help me. Therefore, I will not
let this diagnosis confound me. Instead, I will
set my face like a flint, fully realizing that you
will not allow me to be ashamed.[6]

I ask you to let your peace — a peace that surpasses all understanding — keep my heart and my *mind* (including my memory) through Christ Jesus.[7] I will not be afraid, because I know you have not given me a spirit of fear, but of love, of power, and of a sound mind.[8] Keep my mind sound, dear Father.

Lord God, you are my confidence.[9] I trust you to deliver me from this affliction.[10] Thank you for healing me and for giving me your peace. Truly it does keep my heart from being troubled or afraid.[11]

How I praise you for your wonderful love in my life. Fill me with the Holy Spirit, Father,[12] so that His quickening power will sustain me.[13] In the name of Jesus Christ I come against the enemy's attempts to bring destruction and disorientation, and I claim your promise of abundant life.[14] Thank you, Father, for healing me. In Jesus' matchless name I pray, Amen.[15]

References: (1) Jeremiah 33:6; (2) 1 Peter 3:12; (3) Psalms 37:7; (4) Psalms 9:9; (5) Proverbs 16:3; (6) Isaiah 50:7; (7) Philippians 4:7; (8) 2 Timothy 1:7; (9) Proverbs 3:26; (10) Psalms 25:20; (11) John 14:27; (12) Ephesians 5:18; (13) Romans 8:11; (14) John 10:10; (15) John 16:23.

7

Arthritis

*A Healing Prayer to Use When
You Suffer From Arthritis*

Healing Promise: *"Beloved, I pray that you may
prosper in all things and be in health, just as your
soul prospers"* (3 John 2).

Healing Prayer: Dear Lord God, thank you
for your promise to heal me. The pain in my
joints from arthritis has caused me great
suffering, but I believe that you are healing
me from the top of my head to the tip of my
toes. Strengthen my body, Father.[1] I believe
your Word which tells me that you want me to
be in health and to prosper just as my soul
prospers.[2] Thank you, Father.

Have mercy on me, O Lord God, and heal
me.[3] I greatly desire healing of this pain,
Father, so that I might serve you more fully.
As your Word directs, I believe I am receiving
your healing from arthritis, and I know I will
soon be living in complete health again.[4]

You send your Word, Father, and you heal
me.[5] Because I know you are healing me, I lift
up my hands and I receive strength in my
feeble knees. I will make straight paths for my
feet so that I will experience your complete

and total healing from the arthritis that has afflicted me.[6] Thank you for your healing touch in my life, dear God.

Thank you for your Word which assures me that the pain and suffering of arthritis are not your will for me. In the power and authority of your Word, I come against all attempts of the enemy — the evil one — to curse my life with pain and affliction in any form. I resist him, Father, in the name of Jesus Christ.[7]

I reach out for the abundant life Jesus has promised to me.[8] You are my light and my salvation; therefore, I will not fear.[9] Indeed, I rejoice in your healing touch, which is removing my pain, healing me, and making me whole. Thank you, Almighty God. In the wonderful name of Jesus, I pray, Amen.[10]

References: (1) Psalms 29:11; (2) 3 John 2; (3) Psalms 6:2; (4) Mark 11:23-24; (5) Psalms 107:20; (6) Hebrews 12:12-13; (7) James 4:7; (8) John 10:10; (9) Psalms 27:1; (10) John 15:16.

8

Attention Deficit Disorder

A Healing Prayer to Use for ADD/ADHD

Healing Promise: *"Keep my soul, and deliver me; let me not be ashamed, for I put my trust in You. Let integrity and uprightness preserve me, for I wait for You"* (Ps. 25:20-21, NKJV).

Healing Prayer: Heavenly Father, I am sure that this attention deficit disorder is not your will for me. Thank you for revealing your loving will to me through your Word. I refuse to accept this curse from the enemy in my life any longer.

Lord God, keep my soul, and deliver me. Let me not be ashamed, for I have put my total, unswerving trust in you. Let your integrity and uprightness preserve me, for I truly wait for you.[1] Father, sometimes people have misunderstood me because of the attention deficit disorder. I know this is not your will for me. Therefore, I ask you to heal me of ADD/ADHD completely and thoroughly.

Increase my faith, dear God, as I meditate upon your Word.[2] I know that faith is the victory that overcomes the world.[3] Therefore, I will abide in you and let your words abide in me, realizing that whatever I ask you will grant to me.[4] Thank you for showing me that faith comes from hearing, Lord God, and hearing comes from your Word.[5] Send your Word, and heal me.[6]

Hold me by my hand, Father, and speak to me.[7] I will not fear, because I know you are helping me.[8] Thank you so much for the promise of healing in my life. Because of your promises to me I will no longer be confounded. In fact, you are enabling me to remain focused and free of any confusion. Therefore, I have set my face like a flint and I know that I shall not be ashamed.[9] Order my steps in your Word, and do not let any iniquity have dominion over me.[10]

Through learning to reverence you, Father, I have gained wisdom, and knowing you gives me understanding.[11] Give me the spirit of wisdom and revelation in the knowledge of you, O God.[12]

In the mighty name of Christ Jesus my Lord, I resist the devil and he flees from me according to your holy Word.[13] Fill me with the Holy Spirit[14] and help me to walk in the Spirit from this time forward.[15]

I rejoice in your promise to keep me in perfect peace as I keep my mind stayed on you and trust in you.[16] I will keep my mind stayed on you, Father, and I will trust you with all my heart. Thank you for healing me and giving me wholeness. In Jesus' powerful name I pray, Amen.[17]

References: (1) Psalms 25:20-21; (2) Romans 10:17; (3) 1 John 5:4; (4) John 15:7-8; (5) Romans 10:17; (6) Psalms 107:20; (7) Isaiah 41:13; (8) Psalms 22:19; (9) Isaiah 50:7; (10) Psalms 119:133; (11) Proverbs 9:10; (12) Ephesians 1:17; (13) James 4:7; (14) Ephesians 5:18; (15) Galatians 5:25; (16) Isaiah 26:3; (17) John 16:23.

9

Back Problems

*A Healing Prayer to Use When
Suffering From Back Problems*

Healing Promise: *"Trust in the Lord with all your heart, and lean not on your own understanding; in all your ways acknowledge Him, and He shall direct your paths. Do not be wise in your own eyes; fear the Lord and depart from evil. It will be health to your flesh and strength to your bones"* (Prov. 3:5-8, NKJV).

Healing Prayer: Father God, you have created my body, and you know what has happened to my back to cause the pain and discomfort I've been experiencing. Because this is true, I want you to know that I am placing my full trust in you. As I acknowledge you, I know you will direct my paths. Therefore, I will always reverence you and depart from all forms of evil. Thank you for your promise to reward me with health and strength.[1] I claim your promise now as I ask you to heal my back problems.

Have mercy on me, O God. Heal me, for I know that pain is not your will for me.[2] I will praise you with my whole heart, for your lovingkindness and your truth are keeping me.[3] As I cry out to you I know you are hearing me, and you are making me bold with strength in my soul as well as my body.[4] Praise you, Father.

Thank you, God, for perfecting that which concerns me. I know my back troubles concern you as well. Your mercy endures forever, Father, and I ask you not to forsake the work of your hands — my body.[5] Look upon my affliction and pain, and forgive me of all my sins.[6]

My faith does not stand in the wisdom of men, dear God, but in your almighty power to heal me totally and completely.[7] Therefore, with your help, I will walk by faith and live by faith.[8] I believe in you, Father, and I thank you that you are rewarding me with healing of whatever is causing the pains in my back.[9] I give you all the glory for your healing power.

From this time forward I will seek first your kingdom and your righteousness, realizing that, as I do so, you will take care of me and meet my needs.[10] How I praise you, Father, for your promise to supply all my needs according to your riches in glory through Christ Jesus, including the need for healing.[11] I claim that promise for my life both now and for the future.

Father, thank you for the promise of Jesus who clearly contrasted the difference between your goals for my life and those of Satan. Whereas Satan wants me to suffer, you want me to experience your wonderful abundance.[12]

I now cast all my cares upon you, Father, and I resist the devil and all his attacks against me.[13] I receive the abundant life you've promised to me, a life free from pain, as I close this prayer with deep gratitude for all you've done for me. In the precious name of Jesus I pray, Amen.[14]

References: (1) Proverbs 3:5-8; (2) Psalms 6:2; (3) Psalms 138:1-2; (4) Psalms 138:3; (5) Psalms 138:8; (6) Psalms 25:18; (7) 1 Corinthians 2:5; (8) Romans 1:17; (9) Hebrews 11:6; (10) Matthew 6:33; (11) Philippians 4:19; (12) John 10:10; (13) 1 Peter 5:7-9; (14) John 15:16.

10

Barrenness

*A Healing Prayer for a Barren Woman Who
Wants to Have a Child*

Healing Promise: *"He settles the barren woman
in her home as a happy mother of children. Praise
the Lord"* (Ps. 113:9, NIV).

Healing Prayer: Father, I ask you to confirm
your Word to me by settling me in my home as
the happy mother of children.[1] I believe the
promise of your Word which loudly declares to
me that you will give me the desires of my
heart.[2] Dear God, to have a child is a great desire
of my heart, and I believe you will answer my
prayer for a child. Thank you, Father.

Truly, your Word imparts faith to my
heart.[3] In fact, I believe you are able to do
exceedingly abundantly beyond all I can ask
or think, according to your power which is at
work in me by your Spirit.[4] Hallelujah!

I rest in your exceedingly great and
precious promises, Father.[5] I know that
nothing is too hard for you.[6] Therefore, I ask
you now for a baby, because I know that you
are able to perform the same kind of miracle
in my life that you did for barren women in
the Bible.

Thank you for all that you are teaching me as I wait before you. Your way is perfect, O God,[7] and you enable me to mount up with wings like an eagle, as I wait before you.[8] Without any reservation, therefore, I will trust in you with all my heart. I choose not to lean toward my own understanding. Instead, I will acknowledge you in all my ways, and I know you will direct my paths.[9] Thank you for hearing and answering my prayer, dear Father.

Your plans for me are so wonderful — to give me a future and a hope.[10] I claim your promise now as great hope fills my heart with joy. Because your lovingkindness is better than life to me, my lips shall praise you. Thus will I bless you, Father. I will lift up my hands in your name. Thank you for satisfying my soul in every way. My mouth shall praise you with joyful lips.[11]

I look forward to welcoming the child you are giving to me. I dedicate myself to raising this child in the nurture and admonition of you, Lord God.[12] Thank you, Father, for your wonderful love and care. In the wonderful name of Jesus I pray, Amen.[13]

References: *(1) Psalms 113:9; (2) Psalms 37:4; (3) Romans 10:17; (4) Ephesians 3:20; (5) 2 Peter 1:4; (6) Genesis 18:14; (7) Psalms 18:30; (8) Isaiah 40:31; (9) Proverbs 3:5-6; (10) Jeremiah 29:11; (11) Psalms 63:3-5; (12) Ephesians 6:4; (13) John 16:23.*

11

Blood Disorders

A Healing Prayer for Someone With Blood Disorders (including leukemia, hemophilia, septicemia, etc.)

Healing Promise: *"Let us therefore come boldly to the throne of grace, that we may obtain mercy and find grace to help in time of need"* (Heb. 4:16, NKJV).

Healing Prayer: Father God, I love you and I know you love me. Therefore, I ask you to heal me of this blood disorder. You are my all-powerful God.

O God, my Father, I come to your throne of grace with the confidence that comes from knowing that you will give me your grace and mercy to help me in my time of need.[1] Thank you, Lord God. My need at this time is for healing of the blood disorder I've been experiencing. Father, I beseech you to grant me my request for a complete and total healing of _____. I believe this is your will for me, because I know you want me to prosper and be in health even as my soul prospers.[2]

Help me, Father, to rejoice in the hope you've imparted to me, to be patient in tribulation, and to continue instant in prayer before your throne.[3] All of your words are pure, and you are my shield. Therefore, I place all my trust in you.[4] Send your Word, and heal me. Deliver me from this blood disease.[5]

Heal me, O Lord God, and I shall be healed, for you are my praise.[6] I claim your promise to restore health to me, and to heal me of this blood disorder.[7] Thank you for the blood of Jesus Christ which was shed in my behalf to cleanse me of all my sins and to heal me of all sicknesses. I receive your healing power now as I pray.[8] I take joy in knowing that by the stripes of Jesus I was healed.[9] Thank you for healing me, Father.

Father, in the power of your Holy Spirit, your Word, and the blood of Jesus, I come against the enemy's attempts to thwart your purposes in my life through illness. I resist the devil now, and he flees from me.[10] Keep me from all evil, Lord.[11] Watch over me and protect me at all times.[12] Thank you for your loving care and healing power which are at work in my life even as I pray. In the matchless name of Jesus I pray, Amen.[13]

References: (1) Hebrews 4:16; (2) 3 John 2; (3) Romans 12:12; (4) Proverbs 30:5; (5) Psalms 107:20; (6) Jeremiah 17:14; (7) Jeremiah 30:17; (8) Mark 11:24; (9) 1 Peter 2:24; (10) James 4:7; (11) Psalms 23:4; (12) 2 Thessalonians 3:3; (13) John 15:16.

12

Breathing Problems

A Healing Prayer for Someone With Breathing Problems (including colds, bronchitis, pneumonia, sinusitis, emphysema, asthma, lung disease, etc.)

Healing Promise: *"Give attention to my words; incline your ear to my sayings. Do not let them depart from your eyes; keep them in the midst of your heart; for they are life to those who find them, and health to all their flesh"* (Prov. 4:20-22, NKJV).

Healing Prayer: My heavenly Father, thank you for your Word and for all the healing promises it contains. I claim those promises now as I ask you to heal me of my breathing problems. I give attention to your Word and I incline my ear to your sayings. With your help, I will not let them depart from my eyes. I will keep them in the midst of my heart, for I know that they are life and health to me.[1]

I know that you hear me when I pray, dear God.[2] And because this is true, I will continually pray — morning, noon, and evening — to you.[3] I will pray without ceasing and rejoice evermore, because I know you are hearing and answering my prayer.[4] Thank you, Father.

In everything I will give thanks to you, O God, for I know this is your will for me in Christ Jesus.[5] Thank you for calling me to prayer and thanksgiving, for I know you are faithful in fulfilling all your promises to me, including the promise of healing for my breathing disorder.[6] You are so great, Father, and you are greatly to be praised, because you are my refuge,[7] you are my Healer, [8] and my great hope.[9]

Father, you are the breath of life.[10] Help me to breathe the fresh air around me fully and deeply. May you truly be the air I breathe. Every breath I take, I take in you, Lord God.

I come against Satan's attempts to wreak havoc in my life, and I stand steadfast in faith, as I resist his attacks against me.[11] Enable me to experience the abundant life Jesus has promised to me at all times.[12]

As I pray, I receive my healing from your hands and my joy is full.[13] Thank you for healing my breathing problems, dear Father, and for imparting to me the very breath of your life. In Jesus' name I pray, Amen.[14]

References: (1) Proverbs 4:20-22; (2) Psalms 4:3; (3) Psalms 55:17; (4) 1 Thessalonians 5:16-17; (5) 1 Thessalonians 5:18; (6) 1 Thessalonians 5:24; (7) Psalms 48:1-3; (8) Exodus 15:26; (9) Psalms 38:15; (10) Genesis 2:7; (11) 1 Peter 5:9; (12) John 10:10; (13) John 16:24; (14) John 16:23.

13

Cancer

*A Healing Prayer to Use When
Diagnosed With Cancer*

Healing Promise: *"With his stripes we are healed"* (Isa. 53:5).

Healing Prayer: Heavenly Father, I thank you for all the promises of your Word, which proclaim healing to those who are sick. Your Word is truth[1] and it is forever settled in heaven.[2] You tell me in your Word that you have provided healing for me through the stripes of Jesus Christ my Lord.[3] I believe your hands will make me whole[4] because this is the promise of your Word.

Mighty God, I take great joy from your promise that though the afflictions of the righteous may be many, you will deliver me and all your children out of them all.[5] Thank you, God, my Healer.[6]

You are always faithful, Father.[7] You fulfill all your promises and you do not lie.[8] Therefore, I ask you to remove all cancer from my body now as I pray.

Heal me of cancer, O Lord God, and I know I will be healed.[9] Thank you for strengthening me. My heart greatly rejoices and I praise you.[10] You are the Lord God who is healing me.[11] As I reach out to touch the hem of the garment of the Great Physician, Jesus Christ,[12] I believe that I receive healing for this cancer[13] and I believe that you, Father God, are making me whole.

I rejoice in your promise that you will heal me of all my diseases, including cancer.[14] Therefore, I bless you with all my soul, and all that is within me blesses your holy name, Father.[15]

With your help, I will endeavor to keep my heart merry each day, because I know that a merry heart does me good like a medicine.[16] Thank you, Father. I will endeavor to walk in the joy you impart to me, because I know your joy truly is my strength.[17] You fill me with all joy and peace, as I believe your Word, and I abound in hope by the power of the Holy Spirit.[18]

Deliver me from all fear, thoughts, and imaginations the devil would bring to torment me.[19] Through faith in your Word, I now bring every thought, and all reasonings and imaginations regarding this cancer, into captivity to the obedience of Christ who is Lord of all.[20] In the authority of the matchless name of Jesus Christ, I confront cancer and all related fears, and I bind them and command them to stop their efforts against me, now.[21]

Cancer is a name, Father, and your Word says that every name must bow its knee at the mere mention of the name of Jesus.[22] Therefore, Father, in the name of Jesus,[23] through faith in that name,[24] and through the merits of the precious blood of Jesus Christ,[25] I now command all cancer in my body to bow its knee, and to leave my body forever.[26] I ask you, Father, to watch over these words of faith and bring them to pass by your great power.[27]

Your Word imparts faith for healing to my heart.[28] I receive your Word, your strength, and I receive your healing now, as I pray. I know that through Jesus I have been made whole.[29] Thank you, Father.

You have enabled me to have the faith I need to be healed.[30] I believe your healing power is working in me now. My prayer is a prayer of faith based upon your Word and the faith that you have imparted to me by your grace, and I know you are healing me and raising me up through your great power.[31] I receive your health, strength, and healing as I pray now in the name of Jesus my Lord.[32] Thank you, Father.

References: (1) 1 John 17:17; (2) Psalms 119:89; (3) Isaiah 53:5; (4) Job 5:18; (5) Psalms 34:19; (6) Exodus 15:26; (7) Hebrews 10:23; (8) Titus 1:2; (9) Jeremiah 17:14; (10) Psalms 28:7; (11) Exodus 15:26; (12) Matthew 9:21; (13) Mark 11:24; (14) Psalms 103:3; (15) Psalms 103:1; (16)

*Proverbs 17:22; (17) Nehemiah 8:10; (18) Romans 15:13;
(19) Joel 2:32; (20) 2 Corinthians 10:5; (21) Matthew
16:19; (22) Philippians 2:10; (23) John 14:13; (24) Acts
3:16; (25) Revelation 12:11; (26) Mark 11:23; (27)
Jeremiah 1:12; (28) Romans 10:17; (29) Acts 9:34; (30)
Acts 14:9-10; (31) James 5:15; (32) John 15:16.*

14

Childbirth — A Prayer of Blessing

A Healing Prayer of Blessing for Parents Who Are Looking Forward to the Birth of a Child

Healing Promise: *"Children are an heritage of the Lord: and the fruit of the womb is his reward"* (Ps. 127:3).

Healing Prayer: Heavenly Father, as I come to you now in the name of Jesus, I thank you so much for the child you are giving to me. I truly regard this child as an inheritance of your love, a reward from your hands.[1] Thank you, Father. Now I ask that you will be with us during the birthing process.

Let your Holy Spirit abide with us and the baby, and please minister your peace and comfort during the entire labor and delivery process, and afterwards as well. I ask that the labor and delivery will go smoothly without complications.[2]

Keep us from all fear[3] and illness.[4] Be our Deliverer in the unique sense of this childbirth, according to your promise.[5] Help us to focus on you as we go through labor and delivery, because we know that when we keep our minds stayed on you and trust you, you will keep us in perfect peace.[6] What a wonderful promise that is! Thank you for all the promises of your Word, dear Father.

Protect the child you are giving to us. Help our child to be wise; one who will bring great joy to us as parents.[7] Already, this child has brought great happiness into our lives.[8] Father, you are our strength,[9] and I know you will see us through each phase of this exciting time.

Give the medical personnel who will be involved in the delivery of our child your wisdom,[10] strength,[11] and peace.[12] I look forward to the precious gift you're bringing into our lives, and, Father, I thank you that you are able to do exceeding, abundantly above all we could ever ask or think, according to your power that works within us.[13] Hallelujah! In Jesus' incomparable name I pray, Amen.[14]

References: *(1) Psalms 127:3; (2) John 14:16-17; (3) Psalms 27:1; (4) Jeremiah 17:14; (5) Psalms 70:1,5; (6) Isaiah 26:3; (7) Proverbs 23:24; (8) Proverbs 23:24; (9) Habakkuk 3:19; (10) James 1:5; (11) Psalms 28:7; (12) Colossians 3:15; (13) Ephesians 3:20; (14) John 16:23.*

15

Choosing a Doctor

A Prayer for Choosing a Doctor

Healing Promise: *"Trust in the Lord with all thine heart; and lean not unto thine own understanding. In all thy ways acknowledge him, and he shall direct thy paths"* (Prov. 3:5-6).

Healing Prayer: Father God, help me in my choice of a doctor to trust you with all my heart, without leaning on my own understanding. In all my ways, including choosing a doctor, I acknowledge you, and I know you will direct my path to the doctor who is best for me.[1] Because I know you will supply all of my needs according to your riches in glory by Christ Jesus,[2] I express faith to you now that you will meet my need for the right doctor for my situation. Thank you, Father.

Thank you for your faithfulness and your mercy, which are always with me.[3] Your lovingkindness is better than life to me, and I know you will never allow your faithfulness to fail me.[4] Therefore, I ask you to lead me, guide me, and take care of me according to your tender mercies.[5]

I delight myself in you, Lord God, and I know you will give me the desire of my heart, which is to find the right doctor.[6] Therefore, I commit my way to you, trusting completely in you, and I know you will meet this need.[7] As I rest in you, Father, and wait patiently for you, I will neither worry nor fret,[8] because your peace which passes all understanding will guard my heart and mind through Christ Jesus.[9]

Give me sound wisdom and discretion, dear Father, for they will be life to my soul and grace to me.[10] Your wisdom and discretion will let me walk safely so that my foot will not stumble, for you, Lord God, are my confidence.[11] Let your wisdom and discretion direct me in my choice of a doctor and medical caregivers. I trust you, Father, to guide me by your Holy Spirit in all my decisions.[12] In Jesus' name I pray, Amen.[13]

References: (1) Proverbs 3:5-6; (2) Philippians 4:19; (3) Psalms 89:24; (4) Psalms 89:33; (5) Psalms 119:77; (6) Psalms 37:4; (7) Psalms 37:5; (8) Psalms 37:7; (9) Philippians 4:7; (10) Proverbs 3:21-22; (11) Proverbs 3:23-26; (12) John 16:13; (13) John 16:24.

16

Circulatory Problems

A Healing Prayer for Someone Who Is Experiencing Circulatory Problems (including high/low blood pressure, hardening of the arteries, blocked arteries, clotting, embolisms, etc.)

Healing Promise: *"He hears the cry of the afflicted"* (Job 34:28, NKJV).

Healing Prayer: Father God, I truly believe you are hearing my prayer for healing from the circulatory problem I've been experiencing,[1] and I thank you for hearing and answering my prayer. I love you, Father, and I know you will help me to rise above this illness. I thank you for your promise to heal me, and to deliver me. I believe you will satisfy me with total health and long life.[2] Thank you, Lord God.

Thank you for being near to me as I call upon you in truth. It thrills me to know that you are fulfilling my desire for healing even as I pray, and that you will always hear my cry.[3] Thank you, Father. As I call to you, I ask you to show me great and mighty things which I do not know.[4] Teach me your ways, so that I will always be certain to walk in your paths.[5]

From this point forward, Father, I will refuse to be anxious or worried about the circulatory problem that has afflicted me, but through prayer, with thanksgiving, I will make my requests known to you. Even as I do so now, I am experiencing your wonderful peace, which surpasses all understanding. Let it continue to guard my heart and mind through Christ Jesus, I pray.[6] Thank you for your peace, Father, and for healing me of the circulatory problem I had been experiencing.

Thank you for your wonderful love, dear God. I believe your Word which tells me that eye has not seen, nor ear heard the things you have in store for me because I love you.[7] Thank you for the glorious promises of your Word through which I am able to partake of your nature, having escaped the corruption that is in the world through lust.[8]

Your Word tells me that "life is in the blood,"[9] Father. In the name of Jesus I pray for my circulatory system to function in perfect health, to be clear, clean and filled with your life, and to be free from all destruction, so that my body which is your temple, may truly glorify you, Father.

Thank you, Lord God, for enabling me to escape the corruption of all circulatory disorders, and I ask you to keep me completely

free from them from this time forth. In Jesus'
name I pray, Amen.[10]

References: (1) Job 34:28; (2) Psalms 91:14-16; (3)
Psalms 145:18-19; (4) Jeremiah 33:3; (5) Psalms 25:4; (6)
Philippians 4:6-7; (7) 1 Corinthians 2:9; (8) 2 Peter 1:4; (9)
Leviticus 17:11; (10) John 15:16.

17

Claiming God's Healing Promises

*A Prayer to Help You Believe God's Healing
Promises and Receive Healing*

Healing Promise: *"Beloved, I wish above all
things that thou mayest prosper and be in health,
even as thy soul prospereth"* (3 John 2).

Healing Prayer: Mighty God, thank you for
your Word, which is a lamp unto my feet and
a light unto my path.[1] I claim your promises of
healing for my body as I pray to you now. I
rejoice in the fact that you want me to prosper
and to be in health.[2] Thank you, Father.

Thank you for Jesus, the Great Physician,
who was wounded for my transgressions and
bruised for my iniquities. I believe your Word,
dear Father, that with His stripes I am healed.[3]
Thank you for forgiving me of all my iniquities, and healing all my diseases.[4] I receive
your healing power as I pray. In the mighty
name of Jesus my Healer, I ask and I receive,
that my joy may be full.[5] Thank you for
healing me and giving me fullness of joy.

It is wonderful to know that the healing
power of Jesus Christ is available to me today
in just the same way as it was available to
lepers and other sick people in Jesus' day. My

Lord Jesus Christ is the same yesterday, today, and forever.[6] Thank you, Father.

Realizing these things, therefore, I diligently hearken to your voice and to your Word, Father. Help me always to do that which is right in your sight, to give ear to your commandments, and to keep all your statutes. Thank you for the promise of your Word which assures me that you will keep all diseases from me, for you are the Lord God who truly does heal me.[7]

Restore health to me, Father, and heal me of all my wounds.[8] Send your Word and heal me,[9] for I realize that your words are life and health to me.[10] Thank you for the great power of your Word, Father, which is sharper than any two-edged sword and is able to pierce even to the division of soul and spirit, and of joints and marrow, and is a discerner of the thoughts and intents of my heart.[11]

Through the power of your Word and the blood of Jesus, I claim your promise of healing for my body, and I thank you that Jesus is my High Priest who knows how I feel.[12] Therefore, I come boldly to your throne of grace, Father, there to obtain your mercy and to find your grace to bring healing to me.[13] Thank you for healing me, Lord God. In the mighty name of Jesus I pray, Amen.[14]

References: *(1) Psalms 119:105; (2) 3 John 2; (3) Isaiah 53:5; (4) Psalms 103:3; (5) John 16:23-24; (6) Hebrews 13:8; (7) Exodus 15:26; (8) Jeremiah 30:17; (9) Psalms 107:20; (10) Proverbs 4:22; (11) Hebrews 4:12; (12) Hebrews 4:14; (13) Hebrews 4:16; (14) John 16:23.*

18

Diabetes

A Healing Prayer for Someone With Diabetes

Healing Promise: *"For the word of God is living and powerful, and sharper than any two-edged sword, piercing even to the division of soul and spirit, and of joints and marrow, and is a discerner of the thoughts and intents of the heart"* (Heb. 4:12, NKJV).

Healing Prayer: Dear God, I ask you to heal me of diabetes. I know that your Word is living and powerful,[1] so I ask you to send your Word and heal me.[2] I will extol you, O Lord God, for you have lifted me up, and I know you will not let this illness triumph over me.[3] I have cried out to you for healing, Father, and I believe you are healing me now, as I pray.[4] Thank you, mighty God.

It is my earnest desire, Father, to heed your voice diligently at all times, and to do what is right in your sight. Therefore, I will give ear to your commandments and keep your statutes. In so doing, I claim your promise that no disease can come upon me and remain upon me, for you are the God who heals me.[5] This blessed realization fills my soul with joy, dear God.

To you, O God, I lift up my soul. O my Father, I put my trust for healing in you. Let me not be ashamed, and don't let diabetes triumph over me any longer, I pray. I believe, mighty God, that no one who waits on you will be ashamed.[6] Show me your ways, and teach me your paths. Lead me in your truth and teach me, for you are my God and you are my Healer.[7]

Look on my affliction and my pain, and forgive me of all my sins. Keep my soul and deliver me. Let me not be ashamed, for I put my trust in you, dear Father.[8]

Lord God, shine your light upon my life and show me if there are things I need to know about my diet and how I care for my body that will help me to walk free of diabetes. I claim your promise that this weapon of diabetes that has been formed against my body will not prosper, for that is my heritage in the righteousness of Christ.[9]

With all my heart I believe it is not your will for me to suffer from diabetes any longer. Therefore, I ask you to rebuke the devourer for my sake.[10] All the promises of your Word, mighty God, are yes and amen in Jesus Christ unto your glory,[11] and I claim and receive your healing promises now in the wonderful name of Jesus.[12]

Thank you for healing me, Father God, and making all the cells and organs of my body function in perfect health and balance. In Jesus' wonderful name I pray, Amen.[13]

References: (1) Hebrews 4:12; (2) Psalms 107:20; (3) Psalms 25:2; (4) Psalms 30:2; (5) Exodus 15:26; (6) Psalms 25:1-3; (7) Psalms 25:4-5; (8) Psalms 25:18,20; (9) Isaiah 54:17; (10) Malachi 3:11; (11) 2 Corinthians 1:20; (12) John 16:24; (13) John 15:16.

19

Digestive Problems

A Healing Prayer for Someone Suffering From Digestive Problems (including colitis, stomach upsets, diarrhea, diverticulosis, constipation, etc.)

Healing Promise: *"The righteous cry out, and the Lord hears, and delivers them out of all their troubles. The Lord is near to those who have a broken heart, and saves such as have a contrite spirit. Many are the afflictions of the righteous, but the Lord delivers him out of them all"* (Ps. 34:17-19, NKJV).

Healing Prayer: Dear Father, thank you for your Word. I believe all its promises to me. It is so wonderful to know that, when I cry out, you do hear me and deliver me out of all my troubles. Thank you for being near to me, and for your promise to deliver me from all illnesses, including the digestive problem I am now facing.[1]

In the full assurance those promises give to me, I ask you to heal me of the digestive problem of _____, as I pray to you now. Thank you for hearing and answering my prayer, dear God.

Thank you for forgiving me of all my sins, and for healing all my diseases, including this digestive disturbance.[2] This realization makes my heart truly merry, and this does me better than any medicine could ever do.[3] Restore complete health and vitality to me, Father, and heal me of all the effects of the problems I have experienced with my digestive system.[4]

Father, help me to glorify you in my body. Guide me and show me if I need to adjust my diet or reduce any areas of stress in order to allow my digestive system to heal and function properly.

Blessed be your name, Lord God. You are my Father and the Father of my Lord and Savior Jesus Christ. Thank you for being the Father of mercies and the God of all comfort and healing in my life.[5] I thank you for enabling me to triumph through Jesus Christ,[6] for His stripes truly have brought healing to me.[7]

I believe that Jesus Christ is the same yesterday, today, and forever.[8] He is the Great Physician of my body and soul, and I receive His healing touch in my body now as I pray.[9] Thank you for blessing me with healing, dear God. In Jesus' wonderful name I pray, Amen.[10]

References: *(1) Psalms 34:17-19; (2) Psalms 103:3; (3) Proverbs 17:22; (4) Jeremiah 30:17; (5) 2 Corinthians 1:3; (6) 2 Corinthians 2:14; (7) 1 Peter 2:24; (8) Hebrews 13:8; (9) Mark 11:24; (10) John 15:16.*

20

Eating Disorders

A Healing Prayer for Someone Who Suffers From Eating Disorders (including anorexia nervosa and bulimia)

Healing Promise: *"Eat, that you may have strength when you go on your way"* (1 Sam. 28:22, NKJV).

Healing Prayer: Mighty Father, thank you for the gift of food. I pray for your help in learning how to overcome this eating disorder. I know it is not your will for me to suffer in this way. I love you, and I know you love me. Help me to follow your admonition to eat properly so that I will have the strength to follow you and serve you at all times.[1]

Teach me how to eat my bread with joy,[2] because I know you are always faithful in supplying my daily bread and meeting all my needs.[3] Thank you for your promise to supply all of my needs according to your riches in glory, through Christ Jesus.[4] I claim this promise as I ask you to meet my need for healing of my eating disorder of _____.

Help me to remember that it's not what I consume that defiles me. Instead, it is what I speak that does so.[5] Give me clear insights, and let your discretion preserve me.[6] Father, I ask for your healing,[7] your direction,[8] your wisdom,[9] your understanding,[10] and your keeping power.[11] Let the power and deception of all eating disorders be removed from my life. Let their strongholds be pulled down now.[12]

In Christ, I have been set free. Help me to stand fast in the liberty you have provided for me from this eating disorder, so I will never again be entangled with the yoke of bondage to any kind of eating disorder.[13] Thank you for helping and healing me, dear God.

You are my refuge, Father, and underneath me are your everlasting arms. Thrust out the enemy from before me at all times.[14] Keep me from all evil.[15] Thank you for your healing power that is at work in me now. In the glorious name of Jesus I pray.[16] ·

References: (1) 1 Samuel 28:22; (2) Ecclesiastes 9:7; (3) Matthew 6:11; (4) Philippians 4:19; (5) Matthew 15:11; (6) Proverbs 2:11; (7) Luke 4:40; (8) Psalms 143:8; (9) James 1:5; (10) Psalms 119:144; (11) 2 Timothy 1:12; (12) 2 Corinthians 10:4; (13) Galatians 5:1; (14) Deuteronomy 33:27; (15) Psalms 23:4; (16) John 16:24.

21

Elders

A Prayer to Use When Elders Are Coming to Pray for Your Healing

Healing Promise: *"Is any sick among you? Let him call for the elders of the church; and let them pray over him, anointing him with oil in the name of the Lord: And the prayer of faith shall save the sick, and the Lord shall raise him up; and if he have committed sins, they shall be forgiven him"* (James 5:14-15).

Healing Prayer: Father, I will obey you by calling the elders of my church to come and pray over me and anoint me with oil in Jesus' name, because I believe their prayer of faith will bring healing to me, as you have promised in your glorious Word.[1]

Heal me, Lord God, and I shall fully recover, for you are my praise.[2] I believe your healing promises, Father, and I believe that you are the Lord who heals me.[3]

Fill me afresh with the Holy Spirit,[4] for I truly believe that He will give quickening life to my mortal body.[5] I give you thanks, dear Father! Let your abundant grace in my life abound to your glory, as you bring healing to me.[6] I praise you that you are renewing my inner self day by day.[7] Thank you, Father.

Your truths enable me to look not at the things which are seen, but at the things which are not seen, for the things that are seen are temporal, and the things that are not seen are eternal.[8]

Father, I will keep my mind stayed on you and I will trust you, because I believe that you will keep me in perfect peace as I do so.[9] Thank you so much. Indeed, I will trust in you with all my heart, instead of leaning on my own understanding. In all my ways I will acknowledge you and I know you will direct my steps.[10] Thank you, Lord God, my Healer. In the matchless name of Jesus I pray, Amen.[11]

References: (1) James 5:14-15; (2) Jeremiah 17:14; (3) Exodus 15:26; (4) Ephesians 5:18; (5) Romans 8:11; (6) 2 Corinthians 4:15; (7) 2 Corinthians 4:16; (8) 2 Corinthians 4:18; (9) Isaiah 26:3; (10) Proverbs 3:5-6; (11) John 15:16.

22

Foot Problems

*A Healing Prayer for Someone
Who Has Foot Problems*

Healing Promise: *"Return to your rest, O my soul, for the Lord has dealt bountifully with you. For You have delivered my soul from death, my eyes from tears, and my feet from falling"* (Ps. 116:7-8, NKJV).

Healing Prayer: I love you, dear God, because I know you hear my voice and my supplications.[1] Because you have inclined your ear to me, I will call upon you as long as I live.[2] Thank you for dealing so bountifully with me, for delivering my soul from death, my eyes from tears, and my feet from falling.[3] Heal this foot condition now, I pray. Thank you, Father.

You are so gracious and so merciful to me. Therefore, I will walk before you with feet that are completely healed.[4] I shall ever praise you, Father, for I know you are the health of my countenance and my God.[5]

Because I know you are restoring health to my feet, I lift up my hands, and I make straight paths for my feet. I will walk in health and healing, not lameness, because I know you are healing me.[6] Thank you, Lord God.

I will lift up my eyes to the hills — from whence comes my help? My help comes from you, Lord God, for you made the heaven and the earth. Therefore, I know you will not permit my foot to be moved (or hurt) in any way. You keep me, and you never slumber nor sleep. Thank you for being my Keeper and my Healer.[7]

Thank you for your promise to preserve me from all evil. I believe you are preserving my soul from this time forth and forevermore.[8] Thank you for preserving me, protecting me, and healing me, dear God.

You are my Lord God. The words you speak will always come to pass. Perform your Word in my life, dear God,[9] by healing me of this foot condition. Thank you for hearing me and for healing me, Father. In Jesus' name I pray, Amen.[10]

References: (1) Psalms 116:1; (2) Psalms 116:2; (3) Psalms 116:7-8; (4) Psalms 116:9; (5) Psalms 42:11; (6) Hebrews 12:12-13; (7) Psalms 121; (8) Psalms 23:4; (9) Ezekiel 12:25; (10) John 16:23.

23

Gall Bladder

*A Healing Prayer for Someone
With Gall Bladder Problems*

Healing Promise: *"For I will restore health unto thee, and I will heal thee of thy wounds, saith the Lord"* (Jer. 30:17).

Healing Prayer: Dear Lord God, I know you are able to heal me of gall bladder problems, and I believe it is your desire to do so. Therefore, I ask you for a complete and total healing as I claim your promise to restore health unto me and to heal me.[1] When my Lord and Savior Jesus Christ walked on earth He healed every sickness and disease He encountered.[2] I believe He is still doing so today, for He never changes; in fact, He is the same yesterday, today, and forever.[3] Thank you for revealing this truth to me, dear God.

Jesus bore my sins and sicknesses in His own body on the cross, so that I, being dead to sins, should live unto righteousness. With your help, mighty God, I will die completely to sin and always live unto righteousness, and I believe your Word which declares that by Jesus' stripes I was healed.[4] Thank you, Father.

My Lord Jesus was wounded for my transgressions, and He was bruised for my iniquities. The chastisement of my peace was upon Him, and with His stripes I am being healed.[5] I claim this truth for myself as I pray, and I believe you are healing me of gall bladder problems right now. Thank you, Lord God.

Send your Word and heal me. Deliver me from this condition, dear God.[6] I will abide in your Word, for I know that your Word imparts life to me and health to all parts of my flesh.[7] Thank you, Father.

Remove this affliction from me, and heal me completely. Realizing that you are healing me, I will be strong and of good courage. I will not fear illness any longer, for I know you are with me. Thank you for the fact that you will never fail me nor forsake me.[8] In the blessed name of Jesus I pray, Amen.[9]

References: (1) Jeremiah 30:17; (2) Matthew 9:35; (3) Hebrews 13:8; (4) 1 Peter 2:24; (5) Isaiah 53:5; (6) Psalms 107:20; (7) Proverbs 4:20-22; (8) Deuteronomy 31:6; (9) John 15:16.

24

God's Care

*A Healing Prayer to Use When You Need to
Know God Cares About You*

Healing Promise: *"Thou, O Lord, art a shield
for me; my glory, and the lifter up of mine head"*
(Ps. 3:3).

Healing Prayer: O God, you are my shield,
my glory, and the lifter up of my head.[1] Thank
you for being everything to me, and for your
constant care in my life. Because I know you
care for me, I now cast all my cares upon you.[2]
Thank you, Father.

Thank you for making me to lie down in
green pastures and for leading me beside the
still waters. Thank you for restoring my soul.[3]
Your rod and your staff, Lord God, do bring
comfort to me.[4]

Your Word does good to me as I walk
uprightly.[5] Thank you for the peace you
impart to me through Jesus.[6] Knowing that He
has overcome the world gives me great peace,
and it helps me to know how much you care
for me.[7] Thank you, Father.

Father of mercies and God of all comfort,
thank you for your wonderful care and protection in my life.[8] You are my faithful God,

and I know you will keep your covenant and mercy with me.[9] I love you, Father. I will sing of your mercies forever, and I will make known your faithfulness to all generations,[10] because I truly believe, Father, that you will not suffer my foot to be moved and you will never slumber nor sleep.[11]

Thank you for caring for me in so many ways. In the wonderful name of Jesus I pray, Amen.[12]

References: (1) Psalms 3:3; (2) 1 Peter 5:7; (3) Psalms 23:2-3; (4) Psalms 23:4; (5) Micah 2:7; (6) John 14:27; (7) John 16:33; (8) 2 Corinthians 1:3; (9) Deuteronomy 7:9; (10) Psalms 89:1; (11) Psalms 121:3-4; (12) John 16:23.

25

Headaches/Migraines

A Healing Prayer for You to Use When You Are Afflicted With a Headache

Healing Promise: *"Himself took our infirmities and bare our sicknesses"* (Matt. 8:17).

Healing Prayer: Dear God, sometimes the pain associated with headaches has been so intense that I've felt disoriented and even sometimes nauseated. I'm sure this is not your will for me. Therefore, I ask you to consider this affliction and deliver me,[1] as I continue to feed upon the truths and promises of your Word. Heal me, O Lord God, and I know I shall be completely healed.[2]

Your Word is a lamp unto my feet and a light unto my path.[3] Thank you for your Word. Send your Word and heal me, I pray.[4] You are the Lord God who is healing me.[5] Thank you for showing me, dear Father, that you want, above all else, for me to walk in health and prosperity.[6] This is such a wonderful realization to me, and I claim the promise it presents for my life right now.

Your Word assures me that you will bind up that which is broken, and you will strengthen the sick.[7] I receive your strengthening power as I pray. Thank you, Father, for your mighty strength.[8]

Thank you for sending Jesus, who has taken away my infirmities and borne my sicknesses.[9] With His stripes I am healed.[10] I receive my healing now by faith,[11] and I trust in you with all my heart, not leaning to my own understanding any longer. In all my ways I will acknowledge you, Father, and I know you will direct my paths.[12]

Thank you for healing me of headaches, dear God. In the matchless name of Jesus I pray, Amen.[13]

References: (1) Psalms 119:153; (2) Jeremiah 17:14; (3) Psalms 119:105; (4) Psalms 107:20; (5) Exodus 15:26; (6) 3 John 2; (7) Ezekiel 34:16; (8) Psalms 118:14; (9) Matthew 8:17; (10) Isaiah 53:5; (11) Mark 11:24; (12) Proverbs 3:5-6; (13) John 15:16.

26

Healing and Health

*A Healing Prayer to Enable You to Experience
God's Healing and Health in Your Body*

Healing Promise: *"Beloved, I pray that you may
prosper in all things and be in health, just as your
soul prospers"* (3 John 2, NKJV).

Healing Prayer: Heavenly Father, I believe
the promise of your Word which tells me that
you want me to prosper in all things and to be
in health, just as my soul prospers.[1] I claim
this promise now as I pray. Heal me, O God,
and I know I shall be healed.[2] Indeed, you are
the Lord God who heals me.[3] I claim your
promises of healing and health.

Through the stripes of Jesus Christ I am
able to experience your healing power, Father.[4]
Thank you so much for all the great and
precious promises of your Word.[5] Mighty God,
I express faith to you that you are healing me,[6]
making me clean,[7] and imparting wholeness
and health to me.[8] Thank you, Lord God.

I believe all the promises of your Word,
Father. Your Word tells me that Jesus himself
took my infirmities and bore my sicknesses,[9]
and with His stripes I am healed.[10] Thank you
for giving me the faith to believe that you are

providing healing and health to me.[11] I receive my healing by faith.[12] Thank you, Father, for loving me so much.[13] In the mighty name of Jesus I pray, Amen.[14]

References: *(1) 3 John 2; (2) Jeremiah 17:14; (3) Exodus 15:26; (4) Isaiah 53:5; (5) 2 Peter 1:4; (6) Matthew 8:2; (7) Mark 1:40; (8) Matthew 9:21; (9) Matthew 8:17; (10) Isaiah 53:5; (11) Mark 5:28; (12) Mark 11:24; (13) 1 John 4:19; (14) John 16:23.*

27

Hearing Disorders

A Healing Prayer for Someone
Who Suffers From Hearing Impairments

Healing Promise: *"In that day the deaf shall hear the words of the book, and the eyes of the blind shall see out of obscurity and out of darkness. The humble also shall increase their joy in the Lord"* (Isa. 29:18-19, NKJV).

Healing Prayer: Father God, I ask you to hasten the day when the deaf will hear the words of your Book, the day when Lebanon shall be turned into a fruitful field, and the fruitful field be esteemed as a forest.[1] Thank you for your promise to keep me in perfect peace as I keep my mind stayed on you, Father. I will trust in you forever, for in you I find both healing and strength.[2]

Send your Word, and heal me, I ask.[3] Your testimonies are wonderful; therefore, my soul will keep them. When your words enter my being, they give me light and understanding and they bring healing to me.[4]

When Jesus walked the earth He performed many miracles. He healed the blind so that they could see, and He healed the deaf so that they could hear.[5] He is my

Lord and Savior, and He is my Great Physician, and I truly believe He is able and willing to heal me of my hearing disorder, because He is the same yesterday, today, and forever.[6] Thank you for His healing touch in my life, dear God.

In the name of Jesus Christ, therefore, I come against the attempts of the devil to cause me harm. I recognize him as a thief who has come to steal, to kill, and to destroy. How thankful I am for Jesus who has come to give me life, so that I could have it even more abundantly.[7]

I claim this promise now, as I seek your healing power, dear God, and I ask you to give me the abundance of perfect hearing now. I joyfully receive my healing from you now, as I pray,[8] Father, for you are the Lord who heals me.[9] Thank you for your healing love in my life. Thank you for hearing and healing me. In Jesus' glorious name I pray, Amen.[10]

References: *(1) Isaiah 29:17-19; (2) Isaiah 26:3; (3) Psalms 107:20; (4) Psalms 119:130; (5) Matthew 11:5; (6) Hebrews 13:8; (7) John 10:10; (8) John 16:24; (9) Exodus 15:26; (10) John 15:16.*

28

Heart Disease

*A Healing Prayer to Use When You
Are the Victim of Heart Disease*

Healing Promise: *"Now the God of hope fill you
with all joy and peace in believing, that ye may
abound in hope, through the power of the Holy
Ghost"* (Rom. 15:13).

Healing Prayer: Father God, fill me with all
the joy and peace that come from believing so
that I will abound in hope through the power
of the Holy Spirit.[1] Thank you for the comfort
you've given to me in spite of the heart
disease I've experienced. Your Word truly
does quicken me.[2]

Father, I trust in you with all my heart,
without leaning to my own understanding. In
all my ways I will acknowledge you, and I ask
you to direct my paths.[3]

Thank you for my heart. I ask you to heal
it and to repair any damage that it may have
sustained. You are my strength, Lord God,
and I know you will make me to walk in high
places.[4] Thank you, Father. As I wait upon
you, I claim your healing promise to all those
who wait upon you. I believe you are healing

me of heart disease, and I believe that I receive your healing power now, as I pray.[5]

Father, you are so good to me. You are my stronghold in the day of trouble, and I know that you know me.[6] I also know that you are aware of all my needs and are able to meet all of my needs through Christ Jesus.[7] Therefore, I will not let my heart be troubled any longer. I believe in you, Father, and in your willingness to heal me.[8]

I am glad and I rejoice in your mercy, for I know you have heard my prayer and considered my troubles.[9] Strengthen my heart as I wait upon you, Father.[10] You are my strength and my shield. My heart completely trusts in you. Therefore, I know you are helping and healing me. My heart greatly rejoices because you love me and you heal me, Father.[11]

You, Lord God, are the strength of my heart.[12] Continue to minister your strength and healing power to me.[13] O Lord my God, I have cried unto you, and I know you are healing me,[14] for you heal all my diseases.[15] Thank you for your grace which is at work in my life. In Jesus' name I pray, Amen.[16]

References: (1) Romans 15:13; (2) Psalms 119:50; (3) Proverbs 3:5-6; (4) Habakkuk 4:19; (5) Mark 11:24; (6) Nahum 1:7; (7) Philippians 4:19; (8) John 14:1; (9) Psalms 31:7; (10) Psalms 27:14; (11) Psalms 28:7; (12) Psalms 73:26; (13) Psalms 103:3; (14) Psalms 30:2; (15) Psalms 103:3; (16) John 16:23.

29

Hospital Stay

A Prayer While in the Hospital

Healing Promise: *"Peace I leave with you, My peace I give to you; not as the world gives do I give to you. Let not your heart be troubled, neither let it be afraid"* (John 14:27, NKJV).

Healing Prayer: Dear heavenly Father, as I spend time now in the hospital, I thank you for the promises of your Word, which assure me that you will never leave me nor forsake me.[1] Your promise of peace comforts me, and I ask you to minister your peace to me now, as I pray.[2] I rejoice that all of your promises are yes and amen in Christ Jesus.[3]

You are faithful,[4] Lord God, and you watch over your Word to perform it in my life.[5] Father, help me, while I am in the hospital, to keep my mind stayed on you and to trust you, because I know this will give me perfect peace.[6] Let your peace, which surpasses all understanding, guard my heart and mind while I am hospitalized.[7]

Father God, I ask you to take good care of me as I go through the various tests and procedures the doctors have chosen or will choose for me. You supply all my need according to your riches in glory by Christ Jesus, Father.[8] I need for my doctor(s) and the medical staff to provide the best possible medical care to me. Therefore, I ask you to give them special skill, wisdom, mental clarity, knowledge and understanding, as they plan and perform the necessary procedures and provide my care afterward.

Help my doctor(s) and the hospital staff, Father, and give them an attitude of mercy and compassion toward me and all their patients, as they minister in the healing arts. I pray for my doctor(s) and the medical staff, and I ask you to fill them with the knowledge of your will in all wisdom and with the special understanding they need to make all the right decisions regarding my care.[9] Enable them to do their work without confusion.[10] Be with them and guide them, as they study my case and make decisions related to my care. Lift up your countenance upon them and give them peace; let your face shine upon them, and bless them, Lord God, as they perform their important ministry.[11]

You, Father, are my protector,[12] and I ask you to protect me from all infections, viruses, mistakes and errors during my confinement in the hospital

Thank you, Father, for loving me with an everlasting love.[13] Let your perfect love fill me now and cast out all fear.[14] I love you, Lord God, for you are my refuge and my fortress. You are my God and in you I will trust.[15] Because I have set my love upon you, loving Father, I know you will deliver me, answer my prayers, be with me, and satisfy me with long life.[16]

Your mercy, O Lord, is holding me up.[17] When anxious thoughts come, my soul delights in your comforts.[18] You are the Father of mercies and the God of all comfort, and I thank you for comforting me during this time of medical procedures and recovery.[19]

I ask for my recovery to be quick and complete, Father, for I know you will restore health to me and heal me of my wounds.[20] You are the Lord who heals me.[21] During this time, Father, I will wait upon you and I know that you will renew my strength.[22]

If any of my physicians do not know you personally, Lord God, I beseech you to lead them to a saving knowledge of Jesus Christ, who is the way, the truth, and the life.[23] Let me be a witness to others during my hospital stay, Father. Fill me with the Holy Spirit,[24] and let the fruit of the Spirit in my life draw others unto you.[25] Empower me by the Holy Spirit to be an effective witness to hospital staff and other patients while I am here.[26] Nothing would thrill me more, Father, than to be able to lead others to a saving knowledge of Jesus Christ.

Bless my doctor(s) and the hospital staff, and all of their loved ones. All these things I ask in the matchless name of Jesus, Amen.[27]

References: *(1) Hebrews 13:5; (2) John 14:27; (3) 2 Corinthians 1:20; (4) Hebrews 10:23; (5) Jeremiah 1:12; (6) Isaiah 26:3; (7) Philippians 4:7; (8) Philippians 4:19; (9) Colossians 1:9; (10) 1 Corinthians 14:33; (11) Numbers 6:24-26; (12) Psalms 91; (13) Jeremiah 31:3; (14) 1 John 4:18; (15) Psalms 91:2; (16) Psalms 91:14-16; (17) Psalms 94:18; (18) Psalms 94:19; (19) 2 Corinthians 1:3; (20) Jeremiah 30:17; (21) Exodus 15:26; (22) Isaiah 40:31; (23) John 14:6; (24) Ephesians 5:18; (25) Galatians 5:22-23; (26) Acts 1:8; (27) John 16:23.*

30

Hysterectomy

*A Healing Prayer for You to Use After
Undergoing a Hysterectomy*

Healing Promise: *"Now thanks be to God who
always leads us in triumph in Christ, and through
us diffuses the fragrance of His knowledge in every
place"* (2 Cor. 2:14, NKJV).

Healing Prayer: Dear Father, thank you for
your Word, which is such a treasure chest of
golden truths and promises for me to apply to
my situation. I do so now, as I ask you to heal
me, emotionally and physically, from this hysterectomy. Your Word assures me that I shall
not want any good thing,[1] and that you will
always lead me to triumph in Christ.[2] Thank
you, Father.

I will never forget your precepts, for they
are reviving me and giving me greater health.[3]
Send your Word, mighty God, and heal me
completely.[4] O keep my soul, and deliver me.
Let me not be ashamed, for I put my trust in
you.[5] Let your lovely peace — a peace which
surpasses all understanding — keep my heart
and mind through Christ Jesus.[6]

Father, how I thank you for the truth that
you are my refuge and strength — a very

present help in trouble.[7] Thank you for being my God — a Father I can completely depend upon. Look upon my affliction and my pain, and forgive me of all my sins.[8] Fill me with the Holy Spirit.[9] The power of the indwelling Holy Spirit imparts life and strength to me.[10] Thank you, Father, for your great love, and for healing me of all effects of the hysterectomy.

I will praise you, O Lord God, because you have lifted me up. O Lord my God, I cried out to you, and you healed me. O Father, you have brought my soul up from the grave, and you have kept me alive.[11] I thank you, mighty God, that you have turned my mourning into dancing for me. You have removed my sackcloth and have girded me with gladness to the end that my glory may sing praises unto you, and will never again be silent. O Lord my God, I will give thanks to you forever.[12] In Jesus' wonderful name I pray, Amen.[13]

References: *(1) Psalms 34:10; (2) 2 Corinthians 2:14; (3) Psalms 119:93; (4) Psalms 107:20; (5) Psalms 25:20; (6) Philippians 4:7; (7) Psalms 46:1; (8) Psalms 25:18; (9) Ephesians 5:18; (10) Romans 8:11; (11) Psalms 30:3; (12) Psalms 30:11-12; (13) John 15:16.*

31

Incontinence

A Healing Prayer for You to Use When You Are Experiencing Bladder or Bowel Control Problems

Healing Promise: *"For I will restore health unto thee, and I will heal thee"* (Jer. 30:17).

Healing Prayer: Mighty Father, thank you for promising healing to me. I believe that all the promises of your Word are yes and amen in Christ Jesus.[1] Therefore, I now claim your promise of full restoration of my health and complete healing.[2] Thank you for hearing and answering my prayer.

I am convinced that it is not your will for me to suffer from incontinence any longer. Holding fast to the profession of my faith without wavering (because I know you are my faithful Father),[3] I refuse to cast away my confidence in your healing power. I know you are healing me.[4] Thank you, Lord God.

This is the confidence I have in you, Father, that when I ask anything according to your will, I know you hear me. Realizing, then, that you are listening to my prayer, I know you will answer it, because I believe you want me to be healed.[5] I claim this promise of healing now, dear God.

In confidence, I look unto Jesus who is the Author and Finisher of my faith.[6] Thank you for Jesus, who is the Great Physician of my soul and body. It thrills me to know that He never changes, Father, that He is the same yesterday, today, and forever, and is still in the healing business.[7] As a result of the stripes He bore for me, I am able to claim my healing, and I do so now, in His name.[8] Thank you for healing me of incontinence, dear God.

Thank you for saving me through the New Birth provided by Jesus Christ, and for enabling me to overcome the world through faith.[9] I receive my healing by faith,[10] and I will walk by faith and not by sight from this time on.[11] In Jesus' name I pray, Amen.[12]

References: (1) 2 Corinthians 1:20; (2) Jeremiah 30:17; (3) Hebrews 10:23; (4) Hebrews 10:35; (5) 1 John 5:14-15; (6) Hebrews 12:2; (7) Hebrews 13:8; (8) Isaiah 53:5; (9) 1 John 5:4; (10) Mark 11:24; (11) 2 Corinthians 5:7; (12) John 16:23.

32

Insomnia

*A Healing Prayer to Use if You
Suffer From Insomnia*

Healing Promise: *"He gives His beloved sleep"*
(Ps. 127:2, NKJV).

Healing Prayer: Father God, thank you for
your promise which indeed assures me that
you give your beloved sleep.[1] I claim this
promise for myself as I pray. Lord God, lift up
the light of your countenance upon me.[2] You
have put gladness in my heart.[3] Therefore, I
will lie down in peace, and sleep; for you
alone, Father, make me dwell in safety.[4] Thank
you for the promise of a peaceful night's sleep.

Thank you for the words of wisdom I find
in the Bible, Lord God. I will not let them
depart from my eyes, because I know they are
life to my soul.[5] Your wisdom enables me to
walk safely, and it keeps my foot from
stumbling.[6] Your wisdom keeps me from
being afraid when I lie down. It enables my
sleep to be sweet.[7] Thank you for your
promises of wisdom, rest, peace, and a good
night's sleep, dear God.

Thank you for giving me work to do,
Father. I realize that I am able to enjoy sweet

sleep because of my labors.[8] Because you have satisfied my weary soul and you have replenished my energy, I am able to sleep soundly and peacefully.[9] Thank you, Father, for taking care of me.

As I go to bed this evening I will not be anxious about anything. Instead, by prayer and supplication with thanksgiving, I make my requests known unto you, Father. I ask that you would give me a good night's sleep, and that you would let your peace which surpasses all understanding guard my heart and mind through Christ Jesus.[10] Thank you, Lord God, for a good night's sleep. In Jesus' matchless name I pray, Amen.[11]

References: (1) Psalms 127:2; (2) Psalms 4:6; (3) Psalms 4:7; (4) Psalms 4:8; (5) Proverbs 3:19-22; (6) Proverbs 3:23; (7) Proverbs 3:24; (8) Ecclesiastes 5:12; (9) Jeremiah 31:25-26; (10) Philippians 4:6-7; (11) John 15:16.

33

Kidney Disease

A Healing Prayer for You to Use When You Suffer From Kidney Disease (including kidney stones, Bright's disease, nephritis, cystitis, etc.)

Healing Promise: *"Heal me, O Lord, and I shall be healed; save me, and I shall be saved: for thou art my praise"* (Jer. 17:14).

Healing Prayer: O God, thank you for your overwhelming love for me. I rejoice and bask in the fact that you care for me. Therefore, I cast my cares about kidney disease upon you.[1] I know you are both willing and able to heal me, and I ask you to deliver me from this sickness of _____. Rebuke the devourer for my sake, dear Father.[2] Heal me, and I know I shall be completely healed, for you truly are my praise.[3]

I thank you for always being ready to perform your Word in my life.[4] How powerful it is.[5] The power of your Word imparts faith to believe your healing promises.[6] Therefore, Father, it is with joy that I believe your Word and I reach forth and receive healing from you for my kidneys now as I pray.[7]

Thank you for showing me, through your Word, that healing is your children's bread.[8] It is with delight that I partake of your wonderful bread of healing as I pray, dear Father, and I thank you for providing healing for me.

To you I will cry, O Lord, my Rock. I know that you will not be silent to me. You will always hear the voice of my supplications as I cry out to you.[9] Help me to keep my heart merry, dear Father, because I know this will do me far better than any medicine can ever do for me.[10] In fact, you are my healing balm.[11] You are faithful, Father, and I trust you to touch my kidneys, to bring complete and total healing to the disease that has afflicted me and to make me whole.[12]

Thank you, Father, for healing me. In Jesus' name I pray, Amen.[13]

References: (1) 1 Peter 5:7; (2) Malachi 3:11; (3) Jeremiah 17:14; (4) Jeremiah 1:12; (5) Hebrews 4:12; (6) Romans 10:17; (7) John 16:24; (8) Mark 7:27; (9) Psalms 28:1; (10) Proverbs 17:22; (11) Jeremiah 8:22; (12) Matthew 9:22; (13) John 16:23.

34

Language Disorders

*A Healing Prayer for You to Use When You
Suffer From Language Disorders (including
stuttering, aphasia, stammering,
lisping, muteness, etc.)*

Healing Promise: *"A merry heart doeth good like
a medicine: but a broken spirit drieth the bones"*
(Prov. 17:22).

Healing Prayer: Mighty Father, help me to
keep a merry heart so that I can experience
full health and healing from your hands.[1] I am
convinced that all healing comes from you,
and because this is true, I ask you to heal me
of the language disorder of _____.
Thank you for showing me that healing is
your children's bread.[2]

Father, you promise in your Word that
the tongue of a stammerer shall be ready to
speak plainly.[3] If you will do that, you will heal
any speech disorder, for you are not a respecter
of persons.[4]

You are the Lord God who is healing me
even as I pray.[5] Thank you, Father. I claim
your promises of healing through the stripes
of Jesus Christ,[6] who took all of my infirmities
upon himself and carried my sicknesses

away.[7] I believe your healing promise, Father, and it is with joy and confidence that I receive healing from your hands now, as I pray.[8]

I bless you, Lord God, and I will not forget all of your benefits to me.[9] You have forgiven me of all my iniquities and you heal all of my diseases and afflictions, including the language disorder.[10] Thank you so much for redeeming my life from destruction and crowning me with your lovingkindness and your tender mercies. Thank you for satisfying my mouth with good things, and for renewing my youth.[11]

How I praise you that you are the Sun of righteousness who rises with healing in your wings.[12] Indeed, you are the Balm of Gilead.[13] Therefore, I place all my hope in you, Lord God, and I shall ever praise you because you are the health of my countenance and my mighty Father.[14] In Jesus' name I pray, Amen.[15]

References: (1) *Proverbs 17:22;* (2) *Mark 7:27;* (3) *Isaiah 32:4;* (4) *Acts 10:34;* (5) *Exodus 15:26;* (6) *Isaiah 53:5;* (7) *Matthew 8:17;* (8) *John 16:24;* (9) *Psalms 103:2;* (10) *Psalms 103:3;* (11) *Psalms 103:4-5;* (12) *Malachi 4:2;* (13) *Jeremiah 8:22;* (14) *Psalms 42:11;* (15) *John 15:16.*

35

Liver Disease

*A Healing Prayer for You to Use When You
Suffer From a Liver Disease
(including cirrhosis, hepatitis, etc.)*

Healing Promise: *"If you abide in Me, and My
words abide in you, you will ask what you desire,
and it shall be done for you"* (John 15:7, NKJV).

Healing Prayer: O God, my Father, I ask you
to rebuke the devourer for my sake.[1] Remove
this liver disease of _____.
Deliver me from its causes and symptoms I
pray.[2] I believe you are the Lord God who is
healing me.[3] Your Word clearly shows me that
you have provided complete healing and
wholeness for me through the stripes of Jesus
Christ, my Lord.[4] I claim the promise of
healing as I pray, dear God.

I praise you, Father, that Jesus Christ
has taken my infirmities and carried my
sicknesses, including liver disease.[5] I praise
you that He is the same yesterday, today, and
forever.[6] I realize that He was wounded for my
transgressions and bruised for my iniquities.
The chastisement of my peace was upon Him,
and by His stripes I am truly healed.[7] Thank
you, Father.

I ask you to fill my liver with your healing virtue by the quickening, life-giving power of your Holy Spirit, so it will be in perfect health and wholeness.[8] Heal me, O Lord God, and I shall be completely whole, for you are my everlasting praise.[9] I receive the blessed healing you have for me right now,[10] because I know you want me to walk in health. As I hearken to your voice and do what is right in your sight, I know you will keep all diseases from me.[11] Thank you, Father.

I bless you, Lord God, and I will never forget all your wonderful benefits and blessings in my life.[12] You forgive me of all my sins, and you heal me of all my diseases.[13] Thank you and bless you, dear Father, for redeeming my life from destruction and crowning me with your lovingkindness and your tender mercies.[14]

Thank you for healing me of liver disease. In Jesus' name I pray, Amen.[15]

References: (1) Malachi 3:11; (2) Psalms 107:6; (3) Exodus 15:26; (4) Isaiah 53:5; (5) Matthew 8:17; (6) Hebrews 13:8; (7) Isaiah 53:5; (8) Romans 8:11; (9) Jeremiah 17:14; (10) Mark 11:24; (11) Exodus 15:26; (12) Psalms 103:1-2; (13) Psalms 103:3; (14) Psalms 103:4; (15) John 16:23.

36
Longevity

A Healing Prayer for a Long Life

Healing Promise: *"With long life will I satisfy him, and show him my salvation"* (Ps. 91:16).

Healing Prayer: Father, I praise you for your wonderful Word. The entrance of your Word gives me light,[1] Your Word is a lamp unto my feet and a light unto my path.[2] In obedience to your Word, Father, I will give honor to my earthly father and mother, that it may be well with me and I may live long on the earth.[3] Guide me and show me how to give proper honor to my father and mother, Lord God.

Father God, teach me to number my days so that I will apply my heart unto wisdom.[4] Impart your wisdom to me.[5] Give me understanding, and I shall live.[6] Let my soul live, and it shall praise you as long as I live.[7] In my reverential fear of you, I find life, and I know you will prolong my days.[8] Thank you, Father. Reverencing you is a fountain of life to me.[9]

Fill me with the Holy Spirit, Father.[10] As He dwells in me, He will impart life to my mortal body.[11] As I continue to seek you, Lord God, I know you will give me life.[12] I will seek good and not evil, and I know this will prolong my life.[13] Thank you, Father.

I promise not to live unto myself, Father.[14] Instead I will stand fast in you,[15] and live, move, and have my being in you for as long as I live.[16] I set my love upon you, dear Father, and you deliver me. You set me on high because I know your name. With long life you will satisfy me and show me your salvation.[17] Thank you for all the promises of long life which your Word declares to me. In the blessed name of Jesus I pray, Amen.[18]

References: (1) Psalms 119:130; (2) Psalms 119:105; (3) Ephesians 6:1-3; (4) Psalms 90:12; (5) James 1:5; (6) Psalms 119:144; (7) Psalms 119:175; (8) Proverbs 10:27; (9) Proverbs 14:27; (10) Ephesians 5:18; (11) Romans 8:11; (12) Amos 5:6; (13) Amos 5:14; (14) Romans 14:7; (15) 1 Thessalonians 3:8; (16) Acts 17:28; (17) Psalms 91:14,16; (18) John 15:16.

37

Menopause

*A Healing Prayer for You to Use as
You Go Through Menopause*

Healing Promise: *"Hear my prayer, O Lord, and
let my cry come to You. Do not hide Your face from
me in the day of my trouble; Incline Your ear to me;
in the day that I call, answer me speedily"* (Ps.
102:1-2, NKJV).

Healing Prayer: O God, my Father, as I go
through this challenging period in my life I
am glad that you are with me. Hear my
prayer, and let my cry come unto you. How
thankful I am to know that you will answer
me speedily.[1] The glorious promises of your
Word inspire me, and through them I am
reminded that you will never forsake me.[2] Thank
you, Father, for the fact that you will never leave
me nor forsake me.[3] I claim this promise now
and I rejoice in your goodness to me.

Give me your wisdom,[4] as well as greater
understanding[5] as I wait upon you, mighty
Father.[6] I also ask for your peace, which
surpasses all understanding.[7] I cast all of my
cares and worries upon you, because I know
you care for me.[8] Replace the stress and
anxiety in my life with the wonderful peace
Jesus promised,[9] dear Father.

I ask you to bless me with good health and make my soul prosperous[10] so I will be able to serve you more effectively. As I wait upon you, I realize that you are renewing my strength,[11] and my mind.[12] Thank you for your joy which is my strength,[13] and for giving me a merry heart that does me better than any medicine could ever do.[14] Through the indwelling presence of the Holy Spirit, my body is being quickened,[15] and I am experiencing the resurrection power of Jesus Christ, my Lord.[16]

Help me always to remember to rejoice evermore,[17] to pray without ceasing,[18] and to give thanks in everything, because I know this is your will for me.[19] Help me to keep my mind stayed on you at all times, Father God, as I venture through this season of my life, for I know this will give me a perfect peace as I trust in you.[20]

Father God, help me to trust in you with all my heart, not leaning unto my own understanding. I want to acknowledge you in all my ways so that you will direct my every step.[21] Thank you for your grace which is always sufficient for me.[22] It enables me to go through menopause with renewed strength, health, hope, and joy. In the blessed name of Jesus I pray, Amen.[23]

References: *(1) Psalms 102:1-2; (2) Psalms 37:25; (3) Hebrews 13:5; (4) James 1:5; (5) Job 12:12; (6) Psalms 27:14; (7) Philippians 4:7; (8) 1 Peter 5:7; (9) John 14:27; (10) 3 John 2; (11) Isaiah 40:31; (12) Ephesians 4:23; (13) Nehemiah 8:10; (14) Proverbs 17:22; (15) Romans 8:11; (16) Philippians 3:10; (17) 1 Thessalonians 5:16; (18) 1 Thessalonians 5:17; (19) 1 Thessalonians 5:18; (20) Isaiah 26:3; (21) Proverbs 3:5-6; (22) 2 Corinthians 12:9; (23) John 16:23-24.*

38

Multiple Sclerosis

*A Healing Prayer to Use When You Are
Battling Multiple Sclerosis*

Healing Promise: *"And He said to me, 'My
grace is sufficient for you, for My strength is made
perfect in weakness'"* (2 Cor. 12:9, NKJV).

Healing Prayer: Heavenly Father, thank you
for your all-sufficient grace which is clearly at
work in my life right now. During times of
weakness brought on by the multiple
sclerosis, I have truly sensed your strength.[1]
Thank you, dear God.

Now I ask you to heal me completely of
this affliction, because I know it is not your
will for me, for you have clearly said that you
want me to prosper and to be in health as my
soul prospers.[2] I claim this promise from your
Word as I pray.

Your grace, mighty God, is far greater than
any sickness. Hallelujah! Thank you that all of
your promises to me, including promises of
health and healing, are yes and amen in Jesus
Christ my Lord.[3] I believe your Word, which
tells me that healing is your children's bread.[4]
Heal me, Father, as I feed upon your Word.

Thank you for Jesus Christ who has taken my infirmities and carried my diseases, including multiple sclerosis.[5] I praise you that He is the same Healer today that He was yesterday.[6] How my heart thrills at the realization that my Lord and Savior Jesus Christ was wounded for my transgressions and was bruised for my iniquities. I'm so grateful that He took the chastisement of my peace upon himself, and with His stripes I am being healed and I am healed.[7] Thank you, Father.

Heal me, Lord God, and I shall be completely healed. Save me, and I shall be saved, for you are my praise.[8] By faith I now believe and I receive the healing you have for me.[9] I believe your Word which tells me that you want me to walk in health, and as I hearken unto your voice, and do what is right in your sight, you will keep all diseases from me.[10] Thank you for this promise, which I apply to my life now, as I pray to you.

Father, my soul blesses you, and I promise never to forget your multitude of benefits and blessings in my life.[11] Thank you for forgiving me of all my iniquities, and healing me of all diseases, including multiple sclerosis.[12]

It gives me such joy to realize that you have redeemed my life from destruction and you have crowned me with your lovingkindness and your tender mercies.[13] In the powerful name of Jesus I pray, Amen.[14]

References: (1) 2 Corinthians 12:9; (2) 3 John 2; (3) 2 Corinthians 1:20; (4) Mark 7:27; (5) Matthew 8:17; (6) Hebrews 13:8; (7) Isaiah 53:5; (8) Jeremiah 17:14; (9) Mark 11:24; (10) Exodus 15:26; (11) Psalms 103:1; (12) Psalms 103:3; (13) Psalms 103:4; (14) John 15:16.

39

Muscle Diseases

A Healing Prayer for You to Use When You Are Afflicted With Muscle Diseases (including muscular dystrophy, myasthenia gravis, myalgia, etc.)

Healing Promise: *"And the prayer of faith shall save the sick, and the Lord shall raise him up; and if he have committed sins, they shall be forgiven him"* (James 5:15).

Healing Prayer: O God, I ask you, in faith, to heal me of the muscle disease and pain I've been experiencing.[1] I know you are able to do exceeding abundantly beyond all I could ever ask or think, according to your healing power which is at work within me.[2] I claim all of your healing promises as I pray, including the promise that assures me that healing has been provided for me through the stripes of Jesus Christ my Lord.[3]

Dear God, you specialize in wonders and miracles, and I ask you for a miracle of healing and total restoration to health. Thank you for declaring and providing your strength to me.[4] I hope in you, Lord God, and I will ever praise you,[5] for you are the God who is healing me.[6] Hallelujah!

Touch my body, I pray, and bring complete and total healing of _____ in my muscles. Strengthen me, Father.[7] Through faith in your name and in your Word I know I will be strong. As I am praying, dear God, I receive the perfect soundness of mind and body you have in store for me.[8] Thank you, Father.

How wonderful it is to know that you are healing me and binding up all my wounds.[9] I will not fear nor be dismayed, because I know that you are with me. You are my God, and, even as I pray, I feel your strength coursing through my muscles. Thank you for helping me, healing me, and upholding me with the right hand of your righteousness.[10]

It gives me great peace and joy, dear Lord God, to know that you are a very present help to me in this time of trouble.[11] Therefore, I cast all my burdens upon you, knowing that you will always sustain me.[12] Thank you for your healing power which is at work in my life, defeating the curse of muscle disease and pain. In Jesus' name, Amen.[13]

References: (1) James 5:15; (2) Ephesians 3:20; (3) Isaiah 53:5; (4) Psalms 77:14; (5) Psalms 42:11; (6) Exodus 15:26; (7) Psalms 28:7; (8) Acts 3:16; (9) Psalms 147:3; (10) Isaiah 41:10; (11) Psalms 46:1; (12) Psalms 55:22; (13) John 16:23.

40

My Doctor(s)

*A Healing Prayer of Gratitude and Support for
You to Pray for Your Physician(s)*

Healing Promise: *"That the God of our Lord
Jesus Christ, the Father of glory, may give to you
the spirit of wisdom and revelation in the
knowledge of Him"* (Eph. 1:17, NKJV).

Healing Prayer: Dear heavenly Father, I thank
you for my doctor(s), and I ask you to give
him/her/them the spirit of wisdom and revelation in the knowledge of Jesus Christ.[1] Dear
God, grant wisdom to my physician(s) so that
he/she/they will be able to do his/her/their
work without confusion.[2] I especially lift up to
you now Dr. _____. Be with him/her as
he/she studies my case and makes decisions
related to my care. Bless him/her, Father.

Show him/her/them your ways, O Lord
God. Teach him/her/them your paths. Lead
him/her/them in truth and teach
him/her/them, I pray.[3] Thank you for the
gifts you've imparted to my physician(s) —
gifts of knowledge, wisdom, and insight.
Help him/her/them to apply those gifts to
my case, dear Father.

Help my physician(s) to understand that your Word is a veritable treasure chest of wisdom, understanding, and knowledge. Lead him/her/them to your Word of truth, dear Father.[4] Make your face to shine upon my doctor(s), Lord God, so that he/she/they will be energized to perform his/her/their important ministry.[5]

If any of my physicians do not know you personally, Lord God, I beseech you to lead them to a saving knowledge of Jesus Christ, who is the way, the truth, and the life.[6] For it is you, dear Father, who imparts wisdom to your children, and out of your mouth proceeds all understanding.[7]

Bless my doctor(s) and his/her/their loved ones, Father. In the wonderful name of Jesus Christ I pray, Amen.[8]

References: (1) Ephesians 1:17; (2) James 1:5; (3) Psalms 25:4-5; (4) John 17:17; (5) Psalms 119:135; (6) John 14:6; (7) Proverbs 2:6-7; (8) John 15:16.

41

My Nurses

*A Healing Prayer of Love and Support for
You to Pray for Your Nurses*

Healing Promise: *"The entrance of Your words gives
light; it gives understanding"* (Ps. 119:130, NKJV).

Healing Prayer: Mighty God, thank you for
the nurses you've sent to minister to my
physical needs and my care. I pray for them
now, because I know they are very busy and
must sometimes feel great stress. I ask you to
bless them with the peace that surpasses all
understanding as they do their important
work.[1] I especially pray for _____,
who seems to need your loving touch in
her/his life in a special way right now.

Father, I ask you to lead each of my nurses
to a saving knowledge of Jesus Christ. Help
each one to know you love them so much that
you sent your only Son to die for them, so
they would experience your abundant and
eternal life.[2] I also ask that you would help
them to order their steps in your Word and
never to let sin have dominion over them.[3]

Impart your wisdom to them, Father, and
help them to see that your wisdom is pure,
peaceable, gentle, and easy to be entreated, full

of mercy and good fruits, without partiality, and without hypocrisy.[4] Let each one know how much you love her/him, dear God.[5]

Give them patience, Father, as they serve so many different people. Help them to know the power and the fruit of your Holy Spirit, which is love, joy, peace, patience, gentleness, goodness, faithfulness, meekness, and self-control.[6] Bless their families, Father, in every possible way. Lead them in such a way that they will give full heed to your Word, because your Word will give them light and understanding as they serve you in the important ministry of nursing.[7] In Jesus' glorious name I pray, Amen.[8]

References: (1) Philippians 4:7; (2) John 3:16; (3) Psalms 119:133; (4) James 3:17; (5) 1 John 4:9; (6) Galatians 5:22-23; (7) Psalms 119:130; (8) John 16:23.

42

Neurological Problems

A Healing Prayer to Use When You Suffer With Neurological Problems (including neuralgia, brain disorders, epilepsy, neurasthenia, neuritis, etc.)

Healing Promise: *"God is our refuge and strength, a very present help in trouble"* (Ps. 46:1, NKJV).

Healing Prayer: Wonderful Father, thank you for being my refuge and my strength as I face these neurological problems.[1] As I pray, I cast the burden of this illness upon you, realizing that you will heal me and sustain me.[2] As I cry out to you right now, I believe you are bringing me out of my distresses caused by the illness of _____.[3] Calm the storm in my life, I pray.[4]

I bless you, O Lord, for you forgive all my iniquities and you heal all my diseases.[5] Thank you for Jesus who took my infirmities and bore my sicknesses[6] and with whose stripes I was healed.[7]

Continuously fill me afresh with the Holy Spirit, Lord God.[8] Let the indwelling Holy Spirit quicken my mortal body making it alive with healing and health[9] as I place my faith and trust in you, Father.

How I praise you for your promise to give power to the faint. You are increasing my strength for which I praise you, Father.[10] I surrender to the ministry of the Holy Spirit in my life, as He guides me into all truth and helps me to walk in healing and health.[11] Thank you for your promise to restore health to me, and to heal me of all my wounds, including this neurological problem.[12]

Father, strengthen my immune system and cause my nerves and all the systems of my body and brain to function properly and to be in health. Stretch forth your hand from above and deliver me.[13] Rebuke the devourer for my sake.[14]

Quicken and deliver me, O Lord God, according to your Word.[15] Thank you for healing me and giving me renewed health and strength. In Jesus' marvelous name I pray, Amen.[16]

References: *(1) Psalms 46:1; (2) Psalms 55:22; (3) Psalms 107:28; (4) Psalms 107:29; (5) Psalms 103:3; (6) Matthew 8:17; (7) Isaiah 53:5; (8) Ephesians 5:18; (9) Romans 8:11; (10) Isaiah 40:29; (11) John 16:13; (12) Jeremiah 30:17; (13) Psalms 138:7; (14) Malachi 3:11; (15) Psalms 119:154; (16) John 15:16.*

43

Nutritional Imbalance

*A Healing Prayer for Someone Who Suffers From
a Nutritional Imbalance (including vitamin
deficiency, malnutrition, dehydration,
high cholesterol, etc.)*

Healing Promise: *"The Lord will hear when I
call unto him"* (Ps. 4:3).

Healing Prayer: Knowing that you are
hearing my prayer, Father, I call out to you for
healing from the nutritional imbalance I've
experienced.[1] I know you are able to heal me,
and I know you want to heal me, for your
Word tells me that you want, above all else,
for me to prosper and be in health, even as my
soul prospers.[2] Thank you for this precious
promise from your Word, which I now claim
and receive by faith.

Blessed are you, O Father, for you are the
Father of mercies and the God of all comfort.[3]
Thank you for comforting me as I battle this
nutritional imbalance of _____.
Thank you, also, for loving me so much that
you have shed your love abroad in my heart
by the Holy Spirit whom you've given to me.[4]

Praise you, Father, for your Word, which
is quick, and powerful, and sharper than any

two-edged sword. It pierces even to the dividing asunder of soul and spirit, and of the joints and marrow, and it is a discerner of the thoughts and intents of my heart.[5] Its promises provide me with hope and confidence, because I know they are all yes and amen in Christ Jesus.[6] Therefore, Father, I claim your promises of healing for the nutritional imbalance I've experienced.

Heal me, and I will be completely healed.[7] Give me your wisdom, Father, with regard to the foods I should and should not be eating.[8] Deliver me from the snare of the fowler.[9] O Lord my God, as I cry unto you, I experience your healing power.[10] Send your Word, heal me completely, and deliver me.[11]

The entrance of your Word into my soul brings healing with it, and it gives me greater understanding and wisdom.[12] Thank you, Father, for providing me with all I need to maintain good, balanced nutrition in my life.[13] Help me to obey you in this area as in all areas of my life.[14] In Jesus' name I pray, Amen.[15]

References: (1) Psalms 4:3; (2) 3 John 2; (3) 2 Corinthians 1:3; (4) Romans 5:5; (5) Hebrews 4:12; (6) 2 Corinthians 1:20; (7) Jeremiah 17:14; (8) James 1:5; (9) Psalms 91:3; (10) Psalms 30:2; (11) Psalms 107:20; (12) Psalms 119:130; (13) Philippians 4:19; (14) Acts 5:29; (15) John 16:23.

44

Obesity

*A Healing Prayer for You to Use When
You Are Struggling With Obesity*

Healing Promise: *"Who his own self bare our
sins in his own body on the tree, that we, being
dead to sins, should live unto righteousness: by
whose stripes ye were healed"* (1 Pet. 2:24).

Healing Prayer: Wonderful Father, I come to
you now, in the name of Jesus, asking you to
help me overcome obesity. Show me what I
need to do in order to defeat this adversary in
my life. Thank you for the stripes of Jesus which
are bringing healing to me as I pray.[1] Heal my
soul and my body of all causes and effects of
obesity. You are the Lord that heals me.[2]

I will sing unto you as long as I live. I will
sing praise to you while I have my being. My
meditation of you shall be sweet, and I shall
be glad in you.[3] Fill me afresh with the Holy
Spirit,[4] that I may experience His quickening
power within me.[5]

It is my earnest desire, dear God, to walk
after the Spirit and not after the flesh.[6]
Therefore, I ask you to help me control my
appetite at all times. Let the fruit of the Holy
Spirit, especially self-control, guide my every
choice.[7]

Help me to resist and endure temptation. Thank you so much for your wonderful promise that you will be faithful to me and will provide a way for me to escape from temptation and this affliction.[8] Through your grace I know both how to be abased, and I know how to abound. Everywhere and in all things I am instructed both to be full and to be hungry, both to abound and to suffer need.[9]

Thank you for your instruction in my life, and thank you for your promise to meet my every need in Christ Jesus, my Lord.[10] I rejoice in your promise that I can do all things through Christ who strengthens me.[11] Thank you for His promise, which I now claim, that He has come to give me life more abundantly.[12]

Father, thank you for the gift of joy. I realize that your joy is my strength in this battle against obesity.[13] Thank you for making me joyful and giving me strength. I now know that I am on the pathway of full recovery from obesity. Thank you, Almighty Father. In Jesus' mighty name I pray, Amen.[14]

References: (1) 1 Peter 2:24; (2) Exodus 15:26; (3) Psalms 104:33-34; (4) Ephesians 5:18; (5) Romans 8:11; (6) Galatians 5:16; (7) Galatians 5:23; (8) 1 Corinthians 10:13; (9) Philippians 4:12; (10) Philippians 4:19; (11) Philippians 4:13; (12) John 10:10; (13) Nehemiah 8:10; (14) John 15:16.

45

Osteoporosis/Bone Disease

*A Healing Prayer to Use When You Suffer From
Osteoporosis or Any Bone Disease*

Healing Promise: *"Have mercy on me, O Lord,
for I am weak; O Lord, heal me, for my bones are
troubled"* (Ps. 6:2, NKJV).

Healing Prayer: Have mercy on me, Lord
God, for I am weak. Heal me of the bone
disease of _____.[1]
It is my deepest desire, Father, to trust in you
with all my heart, and not to lean on my own
understanding. In all my ways I will acknowledge you, and I know you will direct my
paths.[2] As I reverence you and depart from
evil, I know I will experience health in my
body and strength in my bones.[3] Thank you,
Father, for your promise of healing.

As I pray, I claim your promise of health
and healing. How it thrills my heart to realize,
Father, that you desire for me, above all else,
to prosper and be in health, even as my soul
prospers.[4] With joy I believe and receive this
promise as the antidote to bone disease.[5] In
the same way that the virtue of Jesus went
forth to the multitude, and healed them all,[6] I
pray that His virtue would bring complete
healing and wholeness to me, for I know that

Jesus Christ my Lord is the same today as He was yesterday.[7] He truly is the Great Physician in my life. Thank you, Father.

How happy I am to know that Jesus took my sins so that I could live unto righteousness. It is by His shed blood and the stripes He bore for me that I am experiencing your healing power,[8] dear God. Thank you so much. How I love you, Father, and my Lord Jesus, who was wounded because of my transgressions and bruised for my iniquities. The chastisement of my peace was upon Him, and with His stripes I am healed.[9] Thank you, Father, for healing me.

Thank you for restoring health to me, as you have promised.[10] I will attend to your words, and incline my ear to the truths of your Word. I will not let them depart from my eyes. I will keep them in the midst of my heart, because I realize that your Word and your words are life to me, and health to all my flesh and bones.[11]

Father, you keep all my bones and not one of them is broken.[12] Your words are pleasant to my soul, and they are health to my bones.[13] Thank you, Lord God. By faith I can now say that You are the healer of my bones. In the matchless name of Jesus I pray, Amen.[14]

References: *(1) Psalms 6:2; (2) Proverbs 3:5-6; (3) Proverbs 3:7-8; (4) 3 John 2; (5) John 16:24; (6) Luke 6:19; (7) Hebrews 13:8; (8) 1 Peter 2:24; (9) Isaiah 53:5; (10) Jeremiah 30:17; (11) Proverbs 4:20-22; (12) Psalms 34:20; (13) Proverbs 16:24; (14) John 15:16.*

46

Pain

A Healing Prayer to Use When
You Are Experiencing Pain

Healing Promise: *"For I will restore health unto thee, and I will heal thee of thy wounds, saith the Lord"* (Jer. 30:17).

Healing Prayer: Heavenly Father, I thank you for your promise to restore health to me and to heal me,[1] for you are the Lord that heals me.[2] Your Word tells me that a merry heart does good like a medicine,[3] Father, so I ask you to fill me with all joy and peace, as I believe your promises, that I may abound in hope through the power of the Holy Spirit.[4] I believe your Word, Father, and I praise you for your goodness to me, as I rejoice with joy unspeakable and full of glory.[5]

I ask you to heal me of this pain, Father. Heal me, O Lord God, and I shall be healed.[6] Touch me, Father, and make me whole.[7]

I believe that Jesus Christ, the Great Physician, is the same yesterday, today, and forever.[8] I believe your Word which tells me that by the stripes of Jesus I was healed.[9] Through Christ my Savior you restore my health and you heal me of all my wounds, dear God.[10]

Thank you for the healing power of your Word, Father, for you sent your Word and healed them.[11] You have sent your Word to me, and I believe your healing promises. I desire to be healed of all pain. Therefore, as I pray now I ask you to heal me of this pain. I believe that I receive your healing virtue into my body and that your power is removing all pain.[12] I rejoice in your truth that with the stripes of Jesus I am healed.[13]

I firmly believe that nothing shall ever be able to separate me from your love, which is in Christ Jesus my Lord.[14] Thank you for the promise you have declared to me, that you want me to prosper in all things and be in health, even as my soul prospers.[15]

Father, I receive your promises and your peace, for you have said that you will keep me in perfect peace when I keep my mind stayed on you and I trust in you.[16] This I now do as I claim your promises of healing for all pain. In Jesus' name I pray, Amen.[17]

References: *(1) Jeremiah 30:17; (2) Exodus 15:26; (3) Proverbs 17:22; (4) Romans 15:13; (5) 1 Peter 1:8; (6) Jeremiah 17:14; (7) Matthew 14:36; (8) Hebrews 13:8; (9) 1 Peter 2:24; (10) Jeremiah 30:17; (11) Psalms 107:20; (12) Mark 11:24; (13) Isaiah 53:5; (14) Romans 8:38-39; (15) 3 John 2; (16) Isaiah 23:6; (17) John 16:23.*

47

Parkinson's Disease

A Healing Prayer for Someone Who Has Parkinson's Disease

Healing Promise: *"Return to your rest, O my soul, for the Lord has dealt bountifully with you. For You have delivered my soul from death, my eyes from tears, and my feet from falling. I will walk before the Lord in the land of the living. I believed, therefore I spoke"* (Ps. 116:7-10, NKJV).

Healing Prayer: Almighty God, thank you for always dealing bountifully with me and for delivering my soul from death, my eyes from tears, and my feet from falling.[1] What shall I render unto you for all your benefits to me? I will take up the cup of salvation, and I will call upon your name.[2] Heal me of Parkinson's disease, Lord God, and I know I shall be completely healed.[3] Thank you for this great promise from your Word.

I am convinced, dear God, that Parkinson's disease is not your will for me. Therefore, I reach out and take hold of your promises of healing. It is your exceeding great and precious promises that enable me to partake of your nature, Father, and to escape the corruption that is in the world, including the corruption of disease.[4] Thank you, my God.

Realizing that it is impossible to please you without faith, Father, I come to you in the full confidence and assurance that you are there for me, listening to me, and ready to act in my behalf. How I praise you that you are a Rewarder to me, as I place my full trust in you and diligently seek you.[5] Thank you for rewarding my faith by healing me of Parkinson's disease.

Your Word, O God, says that it is through faith and patience that I am able to inherit your promise of healing.[6] Father, fill me with the Holy Spirit and let the power of your Holy Spirit quicken and energize my body with your healing power and remove all causes and symptoms of Parkinson's disease from me.[7] I experience the quickening power of the Holy Spirit even now as I am praying to you.[8] Thank you, Father.

I praise you, Father, for the redeeming work of Jesus Christ, my Lord, who provides healing for me through the stripes He bore. Your Word tells me that by His stripes I was healed.[9] By faith in you, Father God, faith that comes from your Word,[10] I now believe and I receive my total and complete healing of Parkinson's disease.[11] I ask and I receive healing from you, Father, that my joy may be full.[12] Thank you for healing me. In the powerful name of Jesus I pray, Amen.[13]

References: (1) Psalms 116:7-10; (2) Psalms 116:12-14; (3) Jeremiah 17:14; (4) 2 Peter 1:4; (5) Hebrews 11:6; (6) Hebrews 6:12; (7) Ephesians 5:18; (8) Romans 8:11; (9) 1 Peter 2:24; (10) Romans 10:17; (11) Mark 11:24; (12) John 16:24; (13) John 15:16.

48

Quickening of the Holy Spirit

A Healing Prayer to Experience the Life-Giving Power of the Holy Spirit in Your Body

Healing Promise: *"But if the Spirit of Him who raised Jesus from the dead dwells in you, He who raised Christ from the dead will also give life to your mortal bodies through His Spirit who dwells in you"* (Rom. 8:11, NKJV).

Healing Prayer: Mighty God, thank you for the precious promise of your Word, which assures me that you will quicken and give your resurrection life to my mortal body through your Holy Spirit who lives and dwells in me.[1] Continuously fill me afresh with the Holy Spirit, I pray. With thanksgiving I will speak to myself in psalms and hymns and spiritual songs, singing and making melody in my heart unto you, Lord God.[2]

I want to experience your presence and power in every area of my life.[3] Thank you for imparting hope to me, and for shedding your love abroad in my heart by the Holy Spirit whom you have given to me.[4]

How I praise you, Father, for the Holy Spirit who is the Spirit of truth. I believe He is guiding me into all truth,[5] and the truth will make me free.[6] Thank you, Father. As the temple of the Holy Spirit, I will remember that I am yours, Father.[7] It is so wonderful to realize that the Holy Spirit — the Comforter and the Spirit of truth — abides with me forever, and He dwells with me and within me.[8] Thank you for His quickening power in my life, Father.

Let His rivers of living water flow out of me, Father.[9] I receive His power in my life, and I realize that the power of the Holy Spirit will enable me to speak forth your Word with greater boldness and authority.[10] How I praise you, Almighty God, for filling me with the Holy Spirit and allowing me to experience His quickening power in my life at all times. In Jesus' name I pray, Amen.[11]

References: (1) Romans 8:11; (2) Ephesians 5:18-20; (3) Acts 1:8; (4) Romans 5:5; (5) John 16:7; (6) John 8:32; (7) 1 Corinthians 6:19; (8) John 14:16-17; (9) John 7:38; (10) Acts 4:31; (11) John 16:23.

49

Skin Problems

A Healing Prayer for You to Use When You Suffer From Skin Disorders

Healing Promise: *"My son, give attention to my words; incline your ear to my sayings. Do not let them depart from your eyes; keep them in the midst of your heart; for they are life to those who find them, and health to all their flesh. Keep your heart with all diligence, for out of it spring the issues of life"* (Prov. 4:20-23, NKJV).

Healing Prayer: Heavenly Father, thank you for your Word, which is a lamp unto my feet and a light unto my path.[1] I claim its promises of healing for my life, and I ask you to completely heal me of the skin problem of _____, as I give attention to your Word and incline my ear to your sayings. I express faith to you, Father, that your Word is imparting life to me and healing and health to my skin.[2] Thank you, Lord God.

I will seek first your kingdom, Father, and in so doing I realize you will take care of all my needs, including my need for healing.[3] Rebuke the devourer for my sake,[4] and fill me with the Holy Spirit.[5] The indwelling presence of the Holy Spirit is imparting life, quickening power, and healing to me.[6] Thank you, Father.

You have imparted confidence to me, Lord God, that, if I ask anything according to your will, I know you hear me. And because I know you hear me, I also know that I will receive the answer I need from you.[7] Thank you for healing me, Lord God.

Restore health to my skin, Father, and heal me of all its wounds.[8] I know you are my Healer, and you are completely restoring health to my skin.[9] Thank you for desiring, above all else, that I should prosper and be in health even as my soul prospers.[10] By faith I claim this promise for myself right now. Thank you, Almighty God. In the name of Jesus I pray, Amen.[11]

References: *(1) Psalms 119:105; (2) Proverbs 4:20-23; (3) Matthew 6:33; (4) Malachi 3:11; (5) Ephesians 5:18; (6) Romans 8:11; (7) 1 John 5:14-15; (8) Jeremiah 30:17; (9) Jeremiah 17:14; (10) 3 John 2; (11) John 15:16.*

50

Sleep Disorders

*A Healing Prayer for You to Use When You
Suffer From Sleeping Disorders*

Healing Promise: *"Beloved, I wish above all things that thou mayest prosper and be in health, even as thy soul prospereth"* (3 John 2).

Healing Prayer: Mighty God, thank you for the power of your Word in my life. It is a lamp unto my feet and a light unto my path.[1] In your Word you assure me that you want me both to prosper and be in health.[2] Thank you for this blessed promise, Father. I know that you are faithful to me, and, when you speak something to me, you will make it good.[3] Therefore, I ask you to heal me of the sleep disorder of _____.

Thank you for your promise to give your beloved sleep.[4] I claim your promise, as I pray, and I ask you to help me have good sleep at the right times, not too much or too little, but sleep that will take care of my need for rest and give me renewed energy. Restore health unto me, dear Father, and heal me.[5] Consider my affliction, and deliver me, as I walk in the truth of your Word.[6]

I know you are helping me and healing me, Father. Therefore, I will not be confounded.

Instead, I will set my face like a flint. In so doing, I know I will not be ashamed.[7] Let your wonderful peace, which surpasses all understanding, keep my heart and mind through Christ Jesus.[8]

How wonderful it is for me to know that you will keep me in perfect peace, dear God, as I keep my mind stayed on you and trust in you.[9] I claim this promise now as I experience your healing power in my life. I place all my hope in you, mighty God, as I reflect on the fact that you are the health of my countenance and my body, and you are my God forever and ever.[10] Thank you for healing me of the sleep disorder. In Jesus' name I pray, Amen.[11]

References: (1) Psalms 119:105; (2) 3 John 2; (3) Numbers 23:19; (4) Psalms 127:2; (5) Jeremiah 30:17; (6) Psalms 119:153; (7) Isaiah 50:7; (8) Philippians 4:7; (9) Isaiah 26:3; (10) Psalms 42:11; (11) John 16:23.

51

Strength

A Healing Prayer for Physical Strength

Healing Promise: *"The Lord is my strength and song, and he is become my salvation"* (Exod. 15:2).

Healing Prayer: Heavenly Father, I thank you for being my strength and my song.[1] You truly are my strength and my shield,[2] and in your joy I find my strength.[3] Help me to remain quiet and confident at all times, because I realize this gives strength to me.[4] With your help I will endeavor to follow your ways at all times, because I know this will bring strength to me.[5]

Indeed, I will trust in you forever, for you are my everlasting strength.[6] Thank you for allowing me to know you, Father, for I realize that this makes me strong.[7] Fill me with the Holy Spirit,[8] because I know He will quicken my mortal body as He dwells within me.[9] Thank you for all the dynamic promises of your Word, Father.[10]

Lord God, you are my strength,[11] and I know that it is not by might, nor by power, but by your Spirit that I shall prevail.[12] Thank you for His strength in my life, Father. I bless you, O God, for you are my strength, and you teach my hands to war, and my fingers to fight.[13] Therefore, I know I shall be strong.[14]

Thank you for giving your strength to me, Father. In the all-powerful name of Jesus I pray, Amen.[15]

References: *(1) Exodus 15:2; (2) Psalms 28:7; (3) Nehemiah 8:10; (4) Isaiah 30:15; (5) Proverbs 10:29; (6) Isaiah 26:4; (7) Daniel 11:32; (8) Ephesians 5:18; (9) Romans 8:11; (10) 2 Peter 1:4; (11) Habakkuk 3:19; (12) Zechariah 4:6; (13) Psalms 144:1; (14) 2 Corinthians 12:10; (15) John 15:16.*

52

Stroke

A Healing Prayer to Use When You Are the Victim of a Stroke

Healing Promise: *"Though I walk in the midst of trouble, You will revive me; You will stretch out Your hand against the wrath of my enemies, and Your right hand will save me. The Lord will perfect that which concerns me; Your mercy, O Lord, endures forever; do not forsake the works of Your hands"* (Ps. 138:7-8, NKJV).

Healing Prayer: Almighty Father, though I have suffered from the effects of a stroke, I know you will revive me and make me well. Stretch out your mighty hand against the enemy of my soul and body.[1] Rebuke the devourer for my sake.[2] In full faith and confidence, I know that your right hand will save me and heal me.[3] Bring perfect healing to me, Father. Do not forsake the work of your hands.[4]

Thank you for your promise to forgive all my iniquities and to heal all my diseases, including the effects of the stroke.[5] I treasure and claim this promise from your Word. I rejoice that you have promised to perfect that which concerns me, for your mercy endures forever.[6] Thank you, Father.

Restore health to me, and heal me of all my wounds, I pray.[7] Send forth your Word and heal me.[8] Thank you for supplying me with your power and increasing my strength.[9] Endue me with your power and increase my strength, Father.[10] My faith rests not in the wisdom of men, but in your power, O God.[11]

As I wait upon you, I recognize that you are renewing my strength right now, and I fully believe that you will enable me to mount up with wings like an eagle so that I shall be able to run and not be weary and walk without fainting.[12]

I rejoice, Father God, that you are faithful to your promises[13] and you hasten your Word to perform it and bring it to pass.[14] You sent your Son, Jesus Christ, to save me and to open the door to your healing mercy. Jesus himself took my infirmities and bore my sicknesses.[15] With His stripes I am healed.[16]

All things are possible to those that believe,[17] Father, and I do believe the healing promises in your Word.[18] Therefore, it is with joy that I receive healing from you now as I pray.[19] I believe that you are ministering complete healing to my body now by your great power. Hallelujah!

Thank you for healing me of both the causes and the effects of the stroke, dear

Father. I pray in the matchless name of Jesus, Amen.[20]

References: *(1) Psalms 138:7-8; (2) Malachi 3:11; (3) Psalms 108:6; (4) Psalms 138:8; (5) Psalms 103:3; (6) Psalms 138:8; (7) Jeremiah 30:17; (8) Psalms 107:20; (9) Isaiah 40:29; (10) Isaiah 41:10; (11) 1 Corinthians 2:5; (12) Isaiah 40:31; (13) Hebrews 10:23; (14) Jeremiah 1:12; (15) Matthew 8:17; (16) Isaiah 53:5; (17) Mark 9:23; (18) Mark 11:24; (19) John 16:24; (20) John 16:23.*

53

Surgery

A Prayer to Use When You Are Facing Surgery

Healing Promise: *"Be anxious for nothing, but in everything by prayer and supplication, with thanksgiving, let your requests be made known to God; and the peace of God, which surpasses all understanding, will guard your hearts and minds through Christ Jesus"* (Phil. 4:6-7, NKJV).

Healing Prayer: Dear heavenly Father, as I face surgery, I thank you for your promise which assures me that your peace, which surpasses all understanding, will guard my heart and mind through Christ Jesus.[1] I claim this promise through prayer and supplication with thanksgiving, and through the peace you give me, I will not be anxious or fretful about the surgery I face.[2]

Your Word assures me that you will never leave me nor forsake me.[3] Your promise of peace comforts me and I ask you to minister your peace to me now as I pray,[4] for I know that all of your promises are yes and amen in Christ Jesus.[5]

You are faithful,[6] Lord God, and you watch over your Word to perform it in my life.[7] Your Word is truth.[8]

You have promised in your Word, Father, to supply all my need according to your riches in glory by Christ Jesus.[9] One of my greatest needs right now is for my doctor(s) and the medical staff to provide the best possible medical care to me. Therefore, I ask you to give them special skill, wisdom, mental clarity, knowledge and understanding as they plan and perform the surgery and provide my care afterward.

Give them an attitude of mercy and compassion toward me and all their patients as they minister in the healing arts. Dear God, give wisdom to my physician(s)[10] so that he/she/they will be able to do his/her/their work without confusion.[11] I especially lift up to you now, my surgeon, Dr. _____. Be with him/her as he/she studies my case and makes decisions related to my care. Bless him/her, Father.

I ask for this surgery to be successful and without complications and for my recovery to be quick and complete. I pray that the doctors will be amazed at the speed of my recovery, Father, for I know you will restore health to me and heal me of my wounds.[12] You are the Lord who heals me.[13]

Thank you, Father, for loving me with an everlasting love.[14] Let your perfect love fill me now and cast out all fear.[15] I love you, Lord

God, for you are my refuge and my fortress. You are my God and in you I will trust. Because I have set my love upon you, loving Father, I know you will deliver me, answer my prayers, be with me, and satisfy me with long life.[16]

Your mercy, O God, is holding me up.[17] You are the Father of mercies and the God of all comfort, and I thank you for comforting me during this time of surgery and recovery.[18] You are good and your mercy endures forever.[19] When anxieties arise to disturb my peace, I will cast all my cares and worries upon you, because I know you take good care of me.[20]

Thank you for the gifts you've imparted to my physician(s) — gifts of knowledge, wisdom, and insight. Help him/her/them to apply those gifts to my case, dear Father.

If any of my physicians do not know you personally, Lord God, I beseech you to lead them to a saving knowledge of Jesus Christ, who is the way, the truth, and the life.[21] Bless my doctor(s) and his/her/their loved ones.

You go before me to prepare the way for me, Father.[22] I know that you never leave me nor do you forsake me.[23] Therefore I will trust in you,[24] and rest in your everlasting arms[25] as I go successfully through this surgery and recovery. In Jesus' name I pray, Amen.[26]

References: *(1) Philippians 4:7; (2) Philippians 4:6; (3) Hebrews 13:5; (4) John 14:27; (5) 2 Corinthians 1:20; (6) Lamentations 3:23; (7) Jeremiah 1:12; (8) John 17:17; (9) Philippians 4:19; (10) Proverbs 2:6; (11) 1 Corinthians 14:33; (12) Jeremiah 30:17; (13) Exodus 15:26; (14) Jeremiah 31:3; (15) 1 John 4:18; (16) Psalms 91; (17) Psalms 94:18; (18) 2 Corinthians 1:3; (19) 1 Chronicles 16:34; (20) 1 Peter 5:7; (21) John 14:6; (22) Isaiah 52:12; (23) Hebrews 13:5; (24) Psalms 37:5; (25) Deuteronomy 33:27; (26) John 15:16.*

54

Ulcers

*A Healing Prayer for Someone
Who Has Ulcers*

Healing Promise: *"For I will restore health unto thee, and I will heal thee of thy wounds, saith the Lord"* (Jer. 30:17).

Healing Prayer: Heavenly Father, thank you for your promise to restore my health and to heal me.[1] I claim this promise as I ask you to heal me of ulcers. Through the blood of Jesus and the word of my testimony I am empowered to overcome the enemy's attempts to bring destruction, disharmony, and disease to me.[2] Rebuke the devourer for my sake, dear Father.[3] Heal me, and I know I shall be completely healed.[4]

Lord God, thank you for being my Shepherd. Because I know this is true, I know I shall never want for any good thing, including healing.[5] You make me to lie down in green pastures, and you lead me beside the still waters.[6] You restore my soul, and lead me in the paths of righteousness for your name's sake.[7] I am thrilled to know that goodness and mercy shall follow me all the days of my life, and I will dwell in your house forever.[8]

Forgive me of all my iniquities, and heal me, I pray.[9] How I thank you that the law of the spirit of life in Christ Jesus has set me free from the law of sin and death.[10] Because you did not spare your own Son, Father, but delivered Him up for me, I am convinced that you will give all good things to me, including healing of ulcers.[11] Thank you for this promise from your Word, dear Father.

I recognize ulcers as being a work of the enemy in my life. Therefore, I come against him in the mighty name of Jesus Christ my Lord. Thank you, Father, for sending Jesus to destroy all the works of the devil in my life.[12]

In the Name of Jesus, I now resist the devil, and I know he flees from me according to your Word, Father God.[13] Your wonderful promises sustain me.

Father, I will do as you have asked me to do. I will cast all my cares upon you, for I know that you care for me.[14] I will not be anxious about these ulcers or anything else, but, as I come before you in prayer and thanksgiving, I know I have your promise of peace that passes all understanding. Your peace will bring healing to both my body and my soul.[15]

It is such a blessing to know that you want me to prosper and be in health, even as my soul prospers.[16] Thank you for healing me of ulcers, dear God. In the incomparable name of Jesus I pray, Amen.[17]

References: *(1) Jeremiah 30:17; (2) Revelation 12:11; (3) Malachi 3:11; (4) Jeremiah 17:14; (5) Psalms 23:1; (6) Psalms 23:2; (7) Psalms 23:3; (8) Psalms 23:6; (9) Psalms 103:3; (10) Romans 8:2; (11) Romans 8:32; (12) 1 John 3:8; (13) James 4:7; (14) 1 Peter 5:6-7; (15) Philippians 4:6-7; (16) 3 John 2; (17) John 16:23.*

55

Urological Problems

A Healing Prayer for You to Use When You Are Experiencing Urological Problems (including, prostate problems, bladder and urinary tract infections, etc.)

Healing Promise: *"Therefore if the Son makes you free, you shall be free indeed"* (John 8:36, NKJV).

Healing Prayer: Mighty Father, I ask you for complete healing of the urological problem of _____. Thank you for all the promises of your Word, which declare healing to me. You, Father, are my refuge and my fortress. You are my God, and I trust you for total healing. Deliver me from the snare of the fowler, and cover me.

Your truth is my shield and buckler, Father.[1] Thank you for the promise that the truth will make me free.[2] Your Son, my Lord Jesus Christ, is the way, the truth, and the life for me,[3] and when He makes me free, I will be free indeed.[4] How I thank you, Lord God, that He is the same Healer today that He was when He walked the earth.[5]

Through you, Lord God, I know I shall do valiantly.[6] Therefore, I will not fear what the enemy will try to do.[7] Father, I resist the devil's attempts to bring destruction to me.[8] I stand steadfast in faith, trusting your love and healing mercy.[9] I cast all my cares upon you (including the urological problem), because I know you care for me.[10] Thank you, Father.

You are the God who does wonders in my life.[11] Heal me, O God, and I know I shall be completely healed, for you are my praise.[12] Thank you for healing me, and enabling me to walk in the confidence that you want, above all else, for me to prosper and to be in health, even as my soul prospers.[13]

You have completely delivered me, Father, and I will rejoice in you forever.[14] God of grace and glory, I believe the promise of your Word, which assures me that you will perfect, establish, strengthen, and settle me in health.[15] To you be glory and dominion forever and ever. These things I pray in the wonderful name of Jesus, Amen.[16]

References: (1) Psalms 91:1-4; (2) John 8:32; (3) John 14:6; (4) John 8:36; (5) Hebrews 13:8; (6) Psalms 60:12; (7) Psalms 64:1; (8) James 4:7; (9) 1 Peter 5:9; (10) 1 Peter 5:7; (11) Psalms 77:14; (12) Jeremiah 17:14; (13) 3 John 2; (14) Psalms 34:19; (15) 1 Peter 5:10-11; (16) John 15:16.

56

Visual Problems

*A Healing Prayer to Use When You Suffer From
Visual and Eye Problems*

Healing Promise: *"The Lord opens the eyes of the
blind; the Lord raises those who are bowed down;
the Lord loves the righteous"* (Ps. 146:8, NKJV).

Healing Prayer: Father God, I come before
your throne of grace with the confidence that
comes from knowing that you hear and
answer prayer.[1] I cast all my cares upon you
because I know you truly care about me.[2]
Thank you for your love in my life, dear
Father.[3] I seek your healing for the visual
problem of _____.

Continuously fill me afresh with the Holy
Spirit,[4] Father, and I ask for the quickening
power of the Holy Spirit to bring complete
healing to my eyes and my body.[5] I believe
you can heal me,[6] want to heal me,[7] and are
healing me. Thank you, Father. Though the
devil wants me to have visual problems, I
know you want me to be well and to experience the abundant life Jesus has promised to
me.[8] I believe your healing promises to me,
and I receive healing for my eyes right now, as
I pray.[9]

Open my eyes; help me to see clearly at all times.[10] Thank you for Jesus who was commissioned by you to give sight to the blind.[11] I believe He is still healing people today as He did in yesteryear.[12] I will look unto Him for He is the Author and Finisher of my faith.[13] My faith reaches out for all you have in store for me, Father, for complete healing and wholeness.

Thank you for hearing my prayer,[14] and for healing my eyes. Thank you for delivering me from the enemy's schemes against me.[15] I shall continually praise you, Lord God, for you are the health of my countenance and my God forever and ever.[16] I love you, and I know you love me. Bless your name, mighty God, my Father.[17] In Jesus' mighty name I pray, Amen.[18]

References: *(1) Hebrews 4:16; (2) 1 Peter 5:7; (3) Romans 8:37; (4) Ephesians 5:18; (5) Romans 8:11; (6) Matthew 9:35; (7) 3 John 2; (8) John 10:10; (9) Mark 11:24; (10) Psalms 146:8; (11) Isaiah 42:7; (12) Hebrews 13:8; (13) Hebrews 12:2; (14) Psalms 4:3; (15) Psalms 91:3; (16) Psalms 43:5; (17) 1 John 4:19.; (18) John 16:23.*

57

Walking in Health

*A Healing Prayer to Enable
You to Experience Good Health*

Healing Promise: *"Beloved, I pray that you may prosper in all things and be in health, just as your soul prospers"* (3 John 2, NKJV).

Healing Prayer: Mighty Father, my Lord and my God, thank you for promising me prosperity and good health.[1] I claim this promise from your Word as I pray. You are the God who does wonders, and you have declared your strength among your people.[2] Thank you, Father. I will fear no evil, because I know you are always with me.[3]

Help me, Father, to be diligent in heeding your voice and doing what is right in your sight. I will give ear to your commandments and keep all your statutes. Thank you for promising me that you will allow no disease to come my way, because you are the Lord God who heals me.[4] Thank you, Lord God, for all the precious promises of your Word.[5]

I trust and serve you, Almighty God, and as I do so I know you will bless my food and drink. Thank you for promising to take all sickness from my midst.[6] Thank you for blessing me in this way and for keeping me. Make your face to continue to shine upon me. I ask you to be gracious unto me and to lift up your countenance upon me and give me your peace.[7] Thank you, Father, for hearing and answering my prayer.[8]

Thank you for preparing a table before me in the presence of my enemies. You anoint my head with oil, and my cup overflows.[9] Surely goodness and mercy shall follow me all the days of my life, and I will dwell in your house forever.[10] Thank you, Father. In the blessed name of Jesus I pray, Amen.[11]

References: (1) 3 John 2; (2) Psalms 77:14; (3) Psalms 23:4; (4) Exodus 15:26; (5) 2 Peter 1:4; (6) Exodus 23:25; (7) Numbers 6:24-26; (8) Psalms 91:15; (9) Psalms 23:5; (10) Psalms 23:6; (11) John 15:16.

Healing

For

Your

Emotions

Jesus announced in the Gospel of Luke, "The Spirit of the Lord is upon me, because he hath anointed me to preach the gospel to the poor; he hath sent me to heal the brokenhearted, to preach deliverance to the captives, and recovering of sight to the blind, to set at liberty them that are bruised" (Luke 4:18). An important part of Jesus' ministry is to bring healing to the broken-hearted, those with wounded or hurting hearts and souls.

Human emotions and feelings are centered in the human soul — the seat of our mind, feelings, will, and emotions. Our soul is affected by our experiences and relationships, which work together in such a way as to influence our emotional responses in our daily lives.

Sometimes we experience hurts, frustrations, losses, disappointments, fears, and uncertainties, which greatly affect our emotions and feelings. When this happens there is a need for healing within our soul. Such soul-healing is the subject of this section of *Healing Prayers*. These positive topical prayers will promote healing in your life — healing of your hurts, your painful and traumatic experiences, and any influence that may presently be having a negative impact upon your attitudes, emotions, and feelings.

God declares this truth to you: "I will seek that which was lost, and bring again that which was driven away, and will bind up that which was broken, and will strengthen that which was sick" (Ezek. 34:16). This is His promise to you. By praying the personal prayers in this section you will experience the loving care of God and the penetrating power of God's Word to bring healing to your emotions and to your soul.

"Then they cried out to the Lord in their trouble, and He saved them out of their distresses. He sent His word and healed them, and delivered them from their destructions. Oh, that men would give thanks to the Lord for His goodness, and for His wonderful works to the children of men" (Ps. 107:19-21, NKJV).

58

Abandonment

A Healing Prayer to Use When
You Are Feeling Abandoned

Healing Promise: *"Forsake me not, O Lord: O my God, be not far from me"* (Ps. 38:21).

Healing Prayer: Mighty God, my heavenly Father, I have been feeling abandoned lately. Therefore, I ask you not to forsake me, and to be not far from me.[1] I need you, Father, and I believe you will never forget your promises to me.[2] Father, I come to you in the name of Jesus Christ my Lord, and I express faith to you now that you will hasten to help me.[3]

Thank you for all the promises of your precious Word. Though others have forsaken me, I know you will never forsake me nor leave me alone.[4] Thank you, Father. Thank you for loving me and caring for me. I know you will never abandon me nor forsake me.[5]

You, Lord God, are a Father to the fatherless, you care for the widowed and set the solitary in families.[6] Help me to find in my own family, friends, community, or in the Body of Christ that place of family, fellowship, and belonging that will relieve my feelings of abandonment and give me a sense of belonging and being loved.

How I rejoice in the truths of your Word, which assure me that you will never forsake your people for the sake of your great name.[7] I cling to your promise which tells me that you will not cast away the righteous and you will not help evildoers.[8] I believe your Word, Father, and it brings great comfort to me.

With your help, dear God, I will be of good courage. I will not fear nor be afraid, because I know you always go with me, and you will not leave me nor forsake me.[9] Thank you, Father.

Even though family members and friends may forsake me, I know you will lift me up.[10] Dear God, as I reflect on the past, I realize that I've never seen you forsake the righteous.[11] This certainty gives me great peace and comfort. Lord God, you are my Rock.[12] I know that you will never leave me comfortless, and that you will always come to me.[13] Thank you, Father.

Because of your Word, I know that I am not abandoned. I rejoice in this truth, and I actively receive and experience your loving presence, now as I pray. I love you, Father, and I will bless your name forever.[14] In the mighty name of Jesus I pray, Amen.[15]

References: *(1) Psalms 38:21; (2) Deuteronomy 4:31; (3) Psalms 71:12; (4) Hebrews 13:5; (5) Psalms 38:21; (6) Psalms 68:5-6; (7) 1 Samuel 12:22; (8) Job 8:20; (9) Deuteronomy 31:6; (10) Psalms 27:10; (11) Psalms 37:25; (12) Psalms 18:2; (13) John 14:18; (14) Psalms 34:1; (15) John 16:23.*

59

Addictive Behaviors

*A Healing Prayer for Someone Who Is
Struggling With Addictive Behaviors*

Healing Promise: *"Stand fast therefore in the
liberty wherewith Christ hath made us free, and be
not entangled again with the yoke of bondage"*
(Gal. 5:1).

Healing Prayer: Father, the addiction I've
been battling against has truly been a yoke of
bondage around my neck. Your Word declares
that I am free through Christ, but I see that it
is my responsibility to maintain my liberty
in Him.[1] This I will do with the help of the
Holy Spirit.

Thank you for the anointing of Jesus
which breaks every yoke.[2] You anointed Him
to preach the gospel to the poor, to heal the
brokenhearted, to preach deliverance to the
captives, and recovering of sight to the blind.
Thank you for promising to set at liberty those
who are bruised through Christ Jesus.[3]

I receive these truths into my life as I pray,
and I thank you, Father, that the truth does, in
fact, make me free.[4] Your Son, Jesus Christ, has
made me free; therefore, I am free from my
addiction indeed![5] Thank you, Father.

Father God, help me to see the true inner need behind my addiction and to find legitimate ways of meeting that need. Let your spirit of wisdom and revelation enlighten my understanding to see clearly why I do this thing and to know fully how much you love me and want to heal me and set me free.[6]

If there is any unforgiveness, bitterness, evil speaking, hatred of others or myself, wrath, sinful anger, or any other sin within me,[7] reveal it to me now, and I will confess it and repent of it so that you may heal me. As you show me my sins, I will say, "Yes, that is sin," and I will confess them to you as sin and turn from them in deep, heartfelt repentance. I ask your forgiveness for these sins. Thank you, Father, that you are now cleansing me from these sins and all unrighteousness through the blood of Christ.[8]

I rejoice in the knowledge that I have been buried with Christ in His death, and this enables me to walk in newness of life, free from the hold of any addiction.[9] Truly, I repent of the addiction to _____ that has held me back for so long, and I renounce it in the name of Jesus, for your Word reveals to me that every knee must bow (including the "knee" of addiction) at the name of Jesus.[10]

I humble myself before you now, Father.[11] With great confidence, therefore, I come to your throne of grace. I ask for your continuing grace in my life to help me completely overcome this addiction.[12] Strengthen me by your Spirit in my inner self.[13]

I give you praise, Father, for you have delivered me out of all the power of darkness and its addictions, and you have translated me into the Kingdom of your dear Son, Jesus Christ.[14] In the Kingdom of Jesus Christ I am free from all addictions. Thank you, Father, for setting me completely free, and allowing me to enter into the glorious liberty of the children of God.[15]

I now know that I will not be addicted to _____any longer. Thank you for loving me so much, Father.[16] In Jesus' wonderful name I pray, Amen.[17]

References: *(1) Galatians 5:1; (2) Isaiah 58:6; (3) Luke 4:18; (4) John 8:32; (5) John 8:36; (6) Ephesians 1:17-19; (7) Ephesians 4:31-32; (8) 1 John 1:9; (9) Romans 6:1-4; (10) Philippians 2:10; (11) 1 Peter 5:6; (12) Hebrews 4:15-16; (13) Ephesians 3:16; (14) Colossians 1:13; (15) Romans 8:21; (16) 1 John 4:19; (17) John 15:16.*

60

Alcoholism

*A Healing Prayer for Freedom
From Alcoholism*

Healing Promise: *"Wine is a mocker, strong drink is a brawler, and whoever is led astray by it is not wise"* (Prov. 20:1, NKJV).

Healing Prayer: Heavenly Father, in the name of Jesus Christ my Lord, I confess my sins to you and I repent of my addiction to alcohol. Please forgive me for being led astray by it and for falling prey to its power in my life.

Father God, I acknowledge that I need your power[1] and your wisdom[2] to enable me to walk in freedom from alcoholism, which has brought such turmoil and misery to me and others.[3] With your help, mighty God, I will walk in the Spirit, so that I will never again fulfill the lusts and addictions of my flesh.[4]

Fill me with your Spirit now, Father, and release your mighty power within me.[5] Break the hold of alcohol addiction in my life forever. I know the power of your Spirit is a key to victory over alcohol in my life. I want to be spiritually minded at all times, Father, because I know that to be spiritually minded is life and peace for me, but to be carnally minded is death.[6]

Dear God, I declare by faith my breakthrough in this area of my life, and I commit myself to standing fast in the liberty wherewith Christ has made me free. With this in mind, I will never again permit myself to be entangled with the yoke of bondage to alcoholism.[7] I will submit myself to your truth, because I know your truth will make me free.[8] With your help, Father, I will resist all of the enemy's temptations, and I know he will flee from me.[9] Thank you, Lord God.

I realize that without you I can do nothing,[10] but through Christ I can do all things because He truly does strengthen me.[11] I know I can walk free from alcohol, because Jesus is the Lord over every temptation and even the power of alcoholism must bow its knee to Him.[12]

Thank you, Father, for surely setting me free, and for keeping me safe from alcoholism through Christ who is my Deliverer.[13] In Jesus' name I pray, Amen.[14]

References: (1) Ephesians 1:19; (2) James 1:5; (3) Proverbs 20:1; (4) Galatians 5:16; (5) Ephesians 5:18; (6) Romans 8:6; (7) Galatians 5:1; (8) John 8:32; (9) James 4:7; (10) John 15:5; (11) Philippians 4:13; (12) Philippians 2:9-10; (13) Romans 11:26; (14) John 16:23.

61

Anger

A Healing Prayer to Use When Anger Seems to Be Getting the Best of You

Healing Promise: *"He that is slow to anger is better than the mighty"* (Prov. 16:32).

Healing Prayer: Dear God, help me to be slow to anger,[1] because I know that wrath works against your righteousness in my life and the lives of others.[2] Father, with your help I will learn to be swift to hear, slow to speak, and slow to get angry.[3]

I want to be more like you, Lord God, because I know you are always ready to pardon, gracious and merciful. You are slow to anger, and you are of great kindness.[4]

Help me to avoid all sinful anger in my life, and to never let the sun go down upon my wrath.[5] Give me understanding of your ways, Father, so that I will be able to be always slow to wrath and never show forth a hasty spirit.[6]

Through the power of your Spirit I will put away all malice, bitterness, wrath, anger and evil speaking from my life, for it is my desire to be kind, tenderhearted, and forgiving toward others, even as you, Father, have forgiven me for Christ's sake.[7]

Thank you, God, for enabling me to cease from the inappropriate expression of anger and to forsake wrath.[8] I believe all the promises of your Word. Set a watch before my lips, and help me to bridle my tongue.[9]

Fill me with the Holy Spirit[10] so that the fruit of the Spirit will sweeten all of my responses and relationships with your love, peace, joy, longsuffering, kindness, goodness, faithfulness, gentleness, self-control.[11] Thank you, Father. In the mighty name of Jesus I pray, Amen.[12]

References: (1) Proverbs 16:32; (2) James 1:20; (3) James 1:19; (4) Nehemiah 9:17; (5) Ephesians 4:26; (6) Proverbs 14:29; (7) Ephesians 4:31-32; (8) Psalms 37:8; (9) Psalms 141:3; (10) Ephesians 5:18; (11) Galatians 5:22-23; (12) John 15:16.

62

Anxiety

*A Healing Prayer to Use When You
Are Worried and Anxious*

Healing Promise: *"Cast thy burden upon the
Lord, and he shall sustain thee"* (Ps. 55:22).

Healing Prayer: Almighty God, thank you for
your personal invitation for me to cast all my
cares upon you. I do so now, fully believing
that you care for me,[1] and knowing that you
will sustain me.[2] Father, as I pour out my heart
before you I realize that you are my refuge
and my safe place.[3] Thank you for being my
great burden-bearer.[4]

You are my peace.[5] As I keep my mind
stayed upon you, I experience your perfect
peace.[6] Therefore, I will not let my heart be
troubled any longer, and neither will I be
afraid, because Jesus has given me His peace.[7]
Thank you, Father.

Your love removes all fear from my life.[8] I
experience your love as I pray, and I thank
you for the peace it gives to me. Because I
know you are helping me, dear God, I will no
longer be anxious about anything, but in
everything by prayer and supplication I will
always let my requests be made unto you.[9]

Thank you, loving Father, for giving me such an effective way out of anxiety, a way that leads me to know fully your peace which surpasses all understanding. I am so grateful that your peace will guard my heart and mind thorough Christ Jesus.[10] In Jesus' name I pray, Amen.[11]

References: *(1) 1 Peter 5:7; (2) Psalms 55:22; (3) Psalms 62:8; (4) Psalms 55:22; (5) Ephesians 2:14; (6) Isaiah 26:3; (7) John 14:27; (8) 1 John 4:18; (9) Philippians 4:6; (10) Philippians 4:7; (11) John 16:23.*

63

Bitterness

*A Healing Prayer to Remove All
Bitterness From Your Life*

Healing Promise: *"Let all bitterness, wrath, anger, clamor, and evil speaking be put away from you, with all malice. And be kind to one another, tenderhearted, forgiving one another, even as God in Christ forgave you"* (Eph. 4:31-32, NKJV).

Healing Prayer: Dear God, thank you for showing me that it is my responsibility to get rid of all bitterness, wrath, anger, clamor, evil speaking, and maliciousness in my life.[1] This I will do, with your powerful help, as I endeavor to be kind, tenderhearted, and forgiving toward others, even as you forgave me in Christ.[2] Thank you, Father.

Fill me afresh with the Holy Spirit,[3] so I will be able to produce the fruit of the Spirit in all the relationships and responsibilities of my life — love, joy, peace, longsuffering, kindness, goodness, faithfulness, gentleness, and self-control.[4]

Restrain my heart from every evil way, including bitterness, as I endeavor to keep your Word.[5] Your Word reminds me that bitterness not only affects me negatively but hurts and defiles those around me as well.[6] I don't want bitterness to have any part in my life, Lord God. I believe that you are teaching me how to overcome bitterness.[7]

Thank you, Father. How sweet your Word is to my taste, Lord God, and it truly does remove all bitterness from me. Your Word is sweeter than honey to my taste.[8] Through your Word I get spiritual understanding; therefore, I hate every false way, including bitterness.[9]

I now take every cause of bitterness in my life, Father, and cast the care of it over onto you, for I know that you care for me.[10] I release all of my bitterness to you, Father, and I refuse to be bitter anymore. I forgive anyone that has in any way hurt or offended me, and I release them from any feeling of bitterness that I have toward them.[11]

I pray, dear Father, that from this day forward, the words of my mouth and the meditations of my heart will always be acceptable in your sight, O Lord God, my strength and my Redeemer.[12] In the incomparable name of Jesus I pray, Amen.[13]

References: (1) Ephesians 4:31; (2) Ephesians 4:32; (3) Ephesians 5:18; (4) Galatians 5:22-23; (5) Psalms 119:101; (6) Hebrews 12:15; (7) Psalms 119:102; (8) Psalms 119:104; (9) Psalms 119:99,104; (10) 1 Peter 5:7; (11) Ephesians 4:32; (12) Psalms 19:14; (13) John 15:16.

64

Broken-Heartedness

*A Healing Prayer to Use When
Your Heart Is Broken*

Healing Promise: *"He heals the broken hearted and binds up their wounds"* (Ps. 147:3, NKJV).

Healing Prayer: O God, I cling to your promise that you heal the broken-hearted and bind up their wounds.[1] As I wait before you, I reach out to you by faith for the healing of my broken heart and all the hurts I've sustained, and I believe that you are making me whole.[2] Your healing touch is very real to me now, as I pray to you. Thank you for your love and tender mercy.[3]

As I come boldly to your throne of grace in my time of healing need,[4] the mighty promises of your Word encourage me and give me strength.[5] Through faith, therefore, I claim your promise that the anointing of your Holy Spirit will bring healing to my broken heart.[6]

Help me to have a merry heart, Lord God, because I know and I believe that a merry heart does one good like a medicine does.[7] In your presence, Father, I experience fullness of joy,[8] and I will rejoice in you always.[9]

When I am cast down and upset, Father, I will hope in you, and I will praise you for helping me to smile again.[10] As David did, I will encourage myself in you.[11]

Heal me, O Lord, and I will be healed, for you are my praise.[12] Thank you for the ongoing ministry of my Lord Jesus Christ, whom you anointed to heal the broken-hearted and to proclaim deliverance to the captives.[13] Father, I express faith to you now that this is happening in my life, and with joy I receive your healing for my broken-hearted-ness.[14] Thank you so much.

Restore my soul.[15] Renew my strength as I wait upon you.[16] Help me to believe fully and to experience the fullness of your promise, that the old things are passed away and you are making all things new in my life.[17] Father, with your help, I will walk in wholeness and renewal from this time forward. Thank you for all that you've done for me and are doing for me.

Father, I purpose to be kind and tender-hearted, forgiving all those who have hurt me.[18] Through your grace, I will walk in love and forgiveness toward them and all others.[19] Thank you for hearing and answering my prayer, dear Father. In the precious name of Jesus I pray, Amen.[20]

References: *(1) Psalms 147:3; (2) Mark 5:34; (3) Psalms 119:77; (4) Hebrews 4:16; (5) Psalms 119:28; (6) Isaiah 61:1; (7) Proverbs 17:22; (8) Psalms 16:11; (9) 1 Thessalonians 5:16; (10) Psalms 42:5; (11) 1 Samuel 30:6; (12) Jeremiah 17:14; (13) Luke 4:18; (14) John 16:24; (15) Psalms 23:3; (16) Isaiah 40:31; (17) 2 Corinthians 5:17; (18) Ephesians 4:32; (19) Ephesians 5:2; (20) John 16:23.*

65

Condemnation

A Healing Prayer to Use When You Are
Experiencing Feelings of Condemnation

Healing Promise: *"There is therefore now no condemnation to those who are in Christ Jesus, who do not walk according to the flesh, but according to the Spirit. For the law of the Spirit of life in Christ Jesus has made me free from the law of sin and death"* (Rom. 8:1-2, NKJV).

Healing Prayer: Heavenly Father, thank you for making me free from the law of sin and death.[1] Help me to fulfill your will for my life by walking according to the Spirit, not according to my flesh.[2] Because I am in Christ Jesus, I know that all condemnation has been removed from me, for the law of the Spirit of life in Christ Jesus has made me free from the law of sin and death.[3] Thank you, Lord God.

Your truth has made me free, dear Father.[4] Thank you for Jesus who is the way, the truth, and the life for me.[5] Thank you for the Spirit of truth[6] who guides me into all truth.[7] Your Word is truth,[8] and I thank you for revealing to me the truth that I never need to feel condemned.[9]

From this time forward I will walk in the truth that I am free from condemnation forever.[10] The liberty you've given to me is glorious indeed.[11] With your help, Father, I will no longer believe the devil's lies when he comes with his accusations, to try to make me feel condemnation.[12]

I will submit myself and my thoughts to you, Father, and I will resist the devil and he will flee from me according to your Word.[13] I will cast down every condemning thought that comes my way, and I will take such thoughts captive unto the obedience of Christ my Lord.[14]

Thank you for enabling me to stand fast in the liberty by which Christ has made me free.[15] I absolutely refuse to be entangled again with the yoke of bondage that condemnation has always brought to me.[16] I am free indeed! Thank you, Father. In the all-powerful name of Jesus I pray, Amen.[17]

References: (1) Romans 8:2; (2) Romans 8:4; (3) Romans 8:1-2; (4) John 8:32; (5) John 14:6; (6) John 15:26; (7) John 16:13; (8) John 17:17; (9) Romans 8:1; (10) 2 John 4; (11) Romans 8:21; (12) Revelation 12:10; (13) James 4:7; (14) 2 Corinthians 10:5; (15) Galatians 5:1; (16) Galatians 5:2; (17) John 15:16.

66

Depression

*A Healing Prayer to Use When
You Are Feeling Depressed*

Healing Promise: *"For I am persuaded, that neither death, nor life, nor angels, nor principalities, nor powers, nor things present, nor things to come, nor height, nor depth, nor any other creature, shall be able to separate us from the love of God, which is in Christ Jesus our Lord"* (Rom. 8:38-39).

Healing Prayer: Wonderful God, thank you for the truth that nothing (including depression) shall ever be able to separate me from your love.[1] I choose to wait upon you, O God, realizing that as I do so you will renew my strength. Thank you for your promise that I shall mount up with wings as an eagle, that I shall run and not be weary, and I shall walk and not faint.[2] I claim that promise from your Word right now, Father.

I bless you, Father, for you are my Father and the Father of my Lord and Savior Jesus Christ. You are the Father of mercies, and the God of all comfort. I receive your healing comfort now as I pray, and I ask you to lift this depression from me. As I am healed of this depression, enable me to comfort others with the same comfort I've received from you.[3] Your Word tells me that you comfort those who are cast down, Lord God, and I believe you are comforting me.[4] Thank you, Father.

I believe you are healing my broken heart, and you are binding up all my wounds.[5] Therefore, I will not fear because I know you are with me. You are my God, and you are strengthening me. Thank you for your help, and thank you for upholding me with the right hand of your righteousness.[6] Father, I cast all my cares upon you because I know you care for me.[7]

Be merciful to me, O God, be merciful to me, for my soul trusts in you, and in the shadow of your wings I will make my refuge, until all depression is completely gone. I will cry out to you, because you are the Most High God who performs all things for me. I know you are sending forth your mercy and truth from heaven, and you are delivering me from all depression.[8] Because I set my love upon you, Father, I know you will deliver me, and you lift me up because I know your name.[9]

I will sing of your power and your mercy because you are my defense and my refuge in the day of my trouble.[10] Restore to me the joy of your salvation and uphold me by your Spirit, Father.[11] You show me the path of life, and as I come into your presence, I find fullness of joy and pleasures forever.[12] Thank you, Father, for your wonderful goodness to me. In Jesus' name I pray, Amen.[13]

References: *(1) Romans 8:39; (2) Isaiah 40:31; (3) 2 Corinthians 1:3-4; (4) 2 Corinthians 7:6; (5) Psalms 147:3; (6) Isaiah 41:10; (7) 1 Peter 5:7; (8) Psalms 57:1-3; (9) Psalms 91:14; (10) Psalms 59:16; (11) Psalms 51:12; (12) Psalms 16:11; (13) John 16:24.*

67
Envy

*A Healing Prayer to Use When You Are
Struggling With Envy*

Healing Promise: *"A sound heart is life to the
body, but envy is rottenness to the bones"* (Prov.
14:30, NKJV).

Healing Prayer: O God, help me to remember
that a calm and sound heart is life and health
to my body, and that all envy, jealousy, and all
forms of malice are rottenness to my bones.[1]
Please keep me from all envy. Having your
righteousness is far better than having the
riches of the others.[2]

Therefore, Father, I will seek first your
righteousness and your kingdom, knowing
that as I do so you will take care of all my
needs.[3] Thank you for promising to supply all
of my needs according to your riches in glory
through Christ Jesus.[4] This truth alone helps
me to see the folly of envy.

Help me to be content, dear Father. Thank
you for giving me peace with you through
Jesus Christ, my Lord.[5] Instead of being
envious, dear God, I will let my requests be
made known to you by prayer and supplica-

tion with thanksgiving. This will ensure that I will have your peace in place of envy.

Thank you for your wonderful peace, which surpasses all understanding. Father, I will let your peace guard my heart and mind through Christ Jesus.[6] Thank you, Father.

Instead of envying others, I will meditate on whatever things are true, just, pure, lovely, and of good report.[7] These are the things which I've received from you, Father, and they help me to know that you, the God of peace, will always be with me.[8] Because this is true, I am able to find contentment in whatever state I find myself.[9] Indeed, I can do all things through Christ who strengthens me.[10]

Thank you, Father, for delivering me from envy and replacing that envy with trust in you. In Jesus' name I pray, Amen.[11]

References: (1) *Proverbs 14:30;* (2) *Psalms 37:16;* (3) *Matthew 6:33;* (4) *Philippians 4:19;* (5) *Romans 5:1;* (6) *Philippians 4:6-7;* (7) *Philippians 4:8;* (8) *Philippians 4:9;* (9) *Philippians 4:11;* (10) *Philippians 4:13;* (11) *John 15:16.*

68

Fear

A Healing Prayer to Use When
You Are Feeling Fearful

Healing Promise: *"The Lord is my light and my salvation; whom shall I fear? The Lord is the strength of my life; of whom shall I be afraid?"* (Ps. 27:1).

Healing Prayer: O God, you are my light and my salvation. You are the strength of my life. Because these statements are true, I know that I do not have to walk in fear any longer.[1] The knowledge that you are with me helps lift feelings of fear from me.[2] Not only are you with me, Lord God, but you are also fighting for me.[3] Thank you, Father.

Even if I should have to walk through the valley of the shadow of death, I will fear no evil, because you are with me.[4] I place my unreserved trust in you, Lord God, and this lifts me out of fear.[5] I will put faith in place of my fear.[6] Knowing the truths and promises of your Word, Father, I will not let my heart be troubled and I will not be afraid.[7]

You are my Helper, Lord God. Accepting this truth makes me feel secure and keeps me from fear.[8] Your perfect love for me removes all fear from my life.[9] Thank you, Father, for the truth that you have not given me a spirit of fear, but rather you have given me a spirit of power, and of love, and of a sound mind.[10]

I now realize that I have not received the spirit of bondage to fear, but I have received the spirit of adoption whereby I am able to cry, "Abba, Father."[11] You are my confidence, Abba, Father, and I know I have no reason whatever to fear.[12] In the mighty name of Jesus I pray, Amen.[13]

References: (1) Psalms 27:1; (2) Genesis 26:24; (3) Deuteronomy 3:22; (4) Psalms 23:4; (5) Psalms 56:4; (6) Mark 5:36; (7) John 14:27; (8) Hebrews 13:6; (9) 1 John 4:18; (10) 2 Timothy 1:7; (11) Romans 8:15; (12) Proverbs 3:26; (13) John 16:23.

69

Grief and Mourning

*A Healing Prayer to Use in a
Time of Personal Loss*

Healing Promise: *"Blessed are they that mourn:
for they shall be comforted"* (Matt. 5:4).

Healing Prayer: Heavenly Father, I know you
are the Father of mercies and the God of all
comfort. I ask you to bring comfort to me during
this time of grief and mourning in my life.[1]

Thank you for your promise to bind up
my broken heart,[2] and to bring comfort to me
as I mourn.[3] I believe your Word, and I receive
your comfort as I pray, because I know your
Word brings life and comfort to me.[4]

When I walk through the valley of the
shadow of death, I will fear no evil, because I
know you, Lord God, are with me. Your
Shepherd's rod and staff bring comfort to me.[5]
Thank you, Father, for being my Shepherd.[6]

I know that Jesus is my High Priest, and
He is touched with the feelings of my grief
and mourning. Realizing this, Father, I come
boldly unto your throne of grace, fully
believing it is there that I will receive your
mercy and find your grace to help me in my
time of need.[7]

The promises of your Word help me to know, dear Father, that I have no reason to fear or despair, because I know you are with me. You are my God. You are strengthening me, and upholding me with the right hand of your righteousness.[8] Thank you, Father. Therefore, I ask you to give me beauty in place of ashes and your oil of joy for my mourning. I will wear the garment of praise that you've provided for me.[9]

Father, as I draw closer to you through praise and singing, I receive your gladness and joy, and I know that my mourning and sorrow will flee.[10] You turned David's mourning into dancing and I know that you can do it for me as well.[11]

Your joy, dear God, is my strength during this difficult time.[12] I love you, Father, and I know that you love me. In the wonderful name of Jesus I pray, Amen.[13]

References: *(1) 2 Corinthians 1:3-4; (2) Isaiah 61:1; (3) Matthew 5:4; (4) Psalms 119:50; (5) Psalms 23:4; (6) Psalms 23:1; (7) Hebrews 4:15-16; (8) Isaiah 41:10; (9) Isaiah 61:3; (10) Isaiah 51:11; (11) Psalms 30:11; (12) Nehemiah 8:10; (13) John 15:16.*

70

Guilt

*A Healing Prayer to Remove All
Guilt From Your Life*

Healing Promise: *"If we confess our sins, He is
faithful and just to forgive us our sins and to cleanse
us from all unrighteousness"* (1 John 1:9, NKJV).

Healing Prayer: Lord God, thank you for
showing me that the way to deal with my
guilt is to confess my sins to you in the full
realization that you are always faithful and
just, and you will forgive me of my sins and
cleanse me from all unrighteousness.[1]
Therefore, I now confess to you my sins of:
_____. Thank
you for your forgiveness, and thank you for
cleansing me from all unrighteousness.

I thank you, Father, that you have
removed my transgressions as far from me as
the East is from the West,[2] and your promise is
that you will remember them no more.[3]
Therefore, I, too, forgive myself and purpose
that I will not receive any remembrance that
brings back guilt.

There is, therefore, now no condemnation
to me. Hallelujah! Father, help me always to
walk according to your Spirit instead of

according to my flesh.[4] For the law of the Spirit of life in Christ Jesus has made me free from the law of sin and death.[5] Thank you, Father, for freeing me from guilt, sin, and death. Enable me to stand fast in the liberty wherewith Christ has set me free, and never again to get entangled with a yoke of bondage to guilt.[6] Thank you for freedom, Father.

It is with the full knowledge that you have taken my guilt from me that I now choose to sanctify you, Lord God, in my heart. This will help me to be ready always to give an answer to everyone that asks me a reason for the hope I have within me. Having a good conscience, I will serve you.[7] God, I thank you that you are light, and there is no darkness at all within you.[8] I want to be more like you, walking in the light so that I may have fellowship with other believers, realizing that the blood of Jesus Christ cleanses me from all sin.[9]

Thank you, Father, for letting Jesus be my Advocate with you, [10] and for allowing Him to be the sacrifice for my sins.[11] Because I now know that I am cleansed from all unrighteousness and I am free from all guilt, I promise, Lord God, to keep your Word and I will always endeavor to walk as Jesus walked.[12] In Jesus' incomparable name I pray, Amen.[13]

References: *(1) 1 John 1:9; (2) Psalms 103:12; (3) Hebrews 10:17; (4) Romans 8:1; (5) Romans 8:2; (6) Galatians 5:1; (7) 1 Peter 3:14-16; (8) 1 John 1:5; (9) 1 John 1:7; (10) 1 John 2:1; (11) 1 John 2:1-2; (12) 1 John 2:5-6; (13) John 16:23.*

71

Inferiority Complex

*A Healing Prayer to Use When
You Feel Inferior to Others*

Healing Promise: *"Just as He chose us in Him before the foundation of the world, that we should be holy and without blame before Him in love"* (Eph. 1:4, NKJV).

Healing Prayer: O Lord my God, as I come to you now in the name of my Savior Jesus Christ, I thank you for your Word, which tells me that you chose me in Christ before the world began and have made me holy and blameless before you in love.

I praise you that through your glorious grace you have made me accepted in Christ as your beloved child.[1] Thank you for showing me how much you love me.[2] Indeed, I thank you that you have actually set your love upon me,[3] and your love for me is an everlasting love.[4] I take immense delight in the love you've showered upon me.

Father, your lovingkindness in my life is better than life to me.[5] Thank you for bringing me into your banqueting table, and for unfurling your banner of love over me.[6] As I draw near to you, I sense you are drawing near to me,[7] and this greatly helps me to see myself as a person of value. Thank you, Father.

It's so wonderful to realize that I am your child, dear God.[8] I know that I am fearfully and wonderfully made by your hands.[9] I am valuable to you, Father. Regardless of the negative thoughts I have had about myself, your Word is true, and your Word tells me that I am so valuable that you bought me at a very expensive price,[10] with the precious blood of Jesus Christ my Lord.[11]

It thrills me to realize that I have been born again by the Spirit,[12] and I am a new creation in Christ.[13] I feel very special as I realize that I am the apple of your eye.[14] Thank you so much, Father.

In light of all these truths from your Word, I recognize that there is no reason for me to feel condemned or inferior any longer.[15] I can live in victory over all feelings and thoughts of inferiority, for I know I can do all things through Christ who strengthens me.[16]

You, O Lord God, are a God who is full of compassion. You are gracious, longsuffering, and plenteous in mercy and in truth.[17] I believe that your mercy is everlasting.[18] Thank you for all the blessed promises of your Word.

I ask you to totally deliver me from all feelings of inferiority, Father.[19] I know you have commissioned me to heal the broken-hearted and to preach deliverance to the captives.[20]

Therefore, Father God, I pledge myself to stand fast in the liberty you've imparted to me through Christ, and I promise that I will not permit myself to be entangled with the yoke of bondage to feelings of inferiority ever again.[21]

When thoughts of inferiority try to invade my thinking I will cast those evil, untrue thoughts down. I will take those thoughts captive to the obedience of Christ and the truth of your Word.[22] Thank you for making me free, Father.[23]

Thank you for delivering me from the enemy's deceptions, from all the power of darkness in my life, and transferring me into the kingdom of the Son of your Love,[24] my wonderful Lord and Savior, Jesus Christ, who loved me and gave His life for me.[25] In Jesus' matchless name I pray, Amen.[26]

References: (1) Ephesians 1:4-6; (2) Romans 5:8; (3) Deuteronomy 7:7-8; (4) Jeremiah 31:3; (5) Psalms 63:3; (6) Song of Solomon 2:4; (7) James 4:8; (8) John 1:12; (9) Psalms 139:14; (10) 1 Corinthians 6:20; (11) 1 Peter 1:19; (12) John 3:5; (13) 2 Corinthians 5:17; (14) Deuteronomy 32:10; (15) Romans 8:1; (16) Philippians 4:13; (17)

Psalms 86:5; (18) Psalms 100:5; (19) Psalms 71:2; (20) Luke 4:18; (21) Galatians 5:1; (22) 2 Corinthians 10:5; (23) John 8:32; (24) Colossians 1:13; (25) Galatians 2:20; (26) John 15:16.

72

Insecurity

*A Healing Prayer to Use
When You Feel Insecure*

Healing Promise: *"Whoever trusts in the Lord shall be safe"* (Prov. 29:25, NKJV).

Healing Prayer: O God, my Father, heal me of all feelings of insecurity as I place all my trust in you. I will not lean unto my own understanding. In all my ways I want always to acknowledge you, and I know you will direct my paths.[1] Thank you for your Word, Father, which shows me that you will keep me safe as I learn to trust in you.[2]

You, Lord God, are my shield and my exceeding great reward.[3] You are the horn of my salvation, my high tower, and my refuge.[4] You are also my defense.[5] You are my buckler and my shield as I trust in you,[6] and I know you will deliver me out of the hand of my enemies.[7]

Thank you, Father, for the secure knowledge that your hand is upon me for good,[8] and goodness and mercy shall follow me all the days of my life, and I will dwell in your house forever.[9] These facts impart a sense of great security to me, Father.

Keep me as the apple of your eye, and hide me under the shadow of your wings.[10] You, my mighty Father, are my rock and my fortress. You are my Deliverer and my God. You are my strength, and I will ever trust in you.[11] Truly I find all my security in you.

Your Word tells me that I have been given all things that pertain to life and godliness, through the knowledge of Jesus Christ, and that I am not only called to glory and virtue, but I am equipped for that calling.[12] You make grace abound towards me that having all sufficiency in all things, I may abound to every good work.[13]

I proclaim that I have been set free from all insecurity in my life, because I know Jesus Christ as my Savior and Lord. Therefore, I determine that I will stand fast in the liberty wherewith Christ has set me free, and I will not be entangled any more in the yoke of bondage of insecurity.[14] Instead, I will be strong in you, Lord God, and in the power of your might.[15]

With your help, I will be strong in faith, giving you all the glory, Lord God, because I am fully persuaded that what you have promised me in your Word you are willing and able to perform in my life.[16] Praise you, Almighty God. In the mighty name of Jesus I pray, Amen.[17]

References: *(1) Proverbs 3:5-6; (2) Proverbs 29:25; (3) Genesis 15:1; (4) 2 Samuel 22:3; (5) Psalms 59:17; (6) Psalms 91:4; (7) 2 Kings 17:39; (8) Ezra 8:22; (9) Psalms 23:6; (10) Psalms 17:8; (11) Psalms 28:7; (12) 2 Peter 1:3; (13) 2 Corinthians 9:8; (14) Galatians 5:1; (15) Ephesians 6:10; (16) Romans 4:20-21; (17) John 16:23.*

73

Intimidation

A Healing Prayer to Use When You
Are Feeling Intimidated

Healing Promise: *"The Lord is my helper, and I will not fear what man shall do unto me"* (Heb. 13:6).

Healing Prayer: O heavenly Father, thank you for being my constant helper. Because I know this is true, I will not fear what other people or circumstances shall attempt to do to me.[1] Heal me of the feelings of intimidation I've been experiencing.

You are my light and my salvation, of what then should I be afraid? You are the strength of my life; therefore, I will fear no one.[2] Thank you for these precious, liberating truths, dear Father.

Even if I should have to walk through the valley of the shadow of death, I will fear no evil, because I know you, Lord God, are always with me.[3] How I thank you for this wonderful truth. Thank you that you are with me.[4] Because I know this is true, I will not be afraid, or intimidated by anyone or anything any longer.[5] Neither will I be dismayed.[6]

I place my full trust in you, Father, and as I do so, I determine not to fear what other people can do to me.[7] I trust your Word, mighty God, which tells me, "Be not afraid of him, says the Lord: for I am with you to save you."[8] I believe you are always with me, Father.

Your Word gives me faith to take my stand against all intimidating influences. I am strong in you, Lord God, and in the power of your might.[9] Knowing this, I will be of good courage, for you strengthen my heart as I hope in you.[10]

I know you love me, Father,[11] and you have not given me a spirit of fear, but of power, and of love, and of a sound mind.[12] I resist all fear and intimidation now, in Jesus' name, and I command all fear and intimidation to depart from me. Thank you, O God, for always giving me the victory through my Lord Jesus Christ.[13]

Greater is He that is in me than he that is in the world![14] Hallelujah! Thank you, Father, for revealing this wonderful truth to me, and setting me free from all intimidation. In Jesus' name I pray, Amen.[15]

References: (1) Hebrews 13:6; (2) Psalms 27:1; (3) Psalms 23:4; (4) Matthew 28:20; (5) Jeremiah 1:8; (6) Ezekiel 3:9; (7) Psalms 56:4; (8) Jeremiah 15:20; (9) Ephesians 6:10; (10) Psalms 31:24; (11) John 3:16; (12) 2 Timothy 1:7; (13) 1 Corinthians 15:57; (14) 1 John 4:4; (15) John 15:16.

74

Loneliness

*A Healing Prayer to Use When
You Are Feeling Lonely*

Healing Promise: *"Fear thou not; for I am with thee: be not dismayed; for I am thy God: I will strengthen thee; yea, I will help thee; yea, I will uphold thee with the right hand of my righteousness"* (Isa. 41:10).

Healing Prayer: Dear Father, even though I am experiencing a sense of loneliness in my life at this time, I believe the promise of your Word which tells me that you are with me. For this reason I do not need to fear or be dismayed, because you, my mighty God, will strengthen me, help me, and uphold me with the right hand of your righteousness.[1] Thank you, Father.

With your help, dear God, I will learn to be content with such things as I have, because just knowing that you are with me and that you will never leave me nor forsake me gives me a renewed sense of peace and confidence.[2]

Thank you for Jesus who is with me until the end of the world.[3] How I thank you, Father, that you will never forsake me[4] and you will not leave me comfortless.[5]

Eternal Father, you are my refuge, and I sense that your everlasting arms are beneath me.[6] Through your grace I am fully persuaded that nothing shall ever be able to separate me from your love, Father, which is in Christ Jesus my Lord.[7]

You are lifting all my loneliness from me, Lord God, as I pray unto you, and knowing that you are with me, will not fail me, and never will forsake me gives me renewed strength and courage.[8] Thank you, Father. You are my refuge and my strength, and you are a very present help to me.[9]

As I cast all my cares and loneliness upon you, Father, I realize anew how deeply you love me and how well you care for me.[10] In Jesus' name I pray, Amen.[11]

References: (1) Isaiah 41:10; (2) Hebrews 13:5; (3) Matthew 28:20; (4) 1 Samuel 12:22; (5) John 14:18; (6) Deuteronomy 33:27; (7) Romans 8:39; (8) Deuteronomy 31:6; (9) Psalms 46:1; (10) 1 Peter 5:7; (11) John 16:23.

75

Lust

*A Healing Prayer for Someone Who Struggles
With Lustful Thoughts and Feelings*

Healing Promise: *"Walk in the Spirit, and ye
shall not fulfil the lust of the flesh"* (Gal. 5:16).

Healing Prayer: Heavenly Father, help me to
walk in the Spirit, so that I shall never fulfill
the lusts of my flesh, because I know the flesh
lusts against the Spirit, and the Spirit against
the flesh, and these are contrary to each other.[1]

Thank you for buying me with the price of
Christ's blood and for allowing my body to be
the temple of the Holy Spirit. Therefore,
Father, I realize that I am not my own, and I
want to glorify you in my body and my spirit
because both of these are yours.[2]

Through your grace, I will put off the old
man, which is corrupt according to deceitful
lusts, and I will be renewed in the spirit of my
mind. Help me to put on the new man, which
is created in righteousness and true holiness
after you, O God.[3] In this way I will give no
place to the devil in my life.[4]

Thank you for your promise that you will
not permit any temptation to take me but such

as is common to humanity. Through your faithfulness, dear Father, you will not let me be tempted above my ability to bear it, but you will, with the temptation, also make a way for me to escape.[5] Thank you, Father. I claim this promise for myself in my struggle against lust.

Lord God, I submit my life totally to you. As I resist the devil now, I know he will flee from me.[6] Help me always to remember that the weapons of my warfare are not carnal, but they are mighty through you, Father, to the pulling down of all strongholds, including lust.[7] Thank you for this truth, dear God.

Fill me with the Holy Spirit, Father,[8] so I will be able to exhibit His fruit in all the relationships and responsibilities of my life. In place of lust, therefore, I will walk in love, joy, peace, patience, meekness, kindness, faithfulness, gentleness, and self-control[9] at all times.

I belong to Christ; therefore, I've crucified the flesh with its passions and desires. With your help, Father, I will live in the Spirit and walk in the Spirit.[10] From this time forward I choose to walk in the Spirit, knowing that as I do so, I will not fulfill the lusts of my flesh.[11] In the mighty name of Jesus I pray, Amen.[12]

References: *(1) Galatians 5:16-17; (2) 1 Corinthians 6:19-20; (3) Ephesians 4:22-24; (4) Ephesians 4:27; (5) 1*

Corinthians 10:13; (6) James 4:7; (7) 2 Corinthians 10:4;
(8) Ephesians 5:18; (9) Galatians 5:22-23; (10) Galatians
5:25; (11) Galatians 5:16; (12) John 15:16.

76

Negative Self-Concept

*A Healing Prayer for Someone Who Has a
Negative Self-Concept*

Healing Promise: *"I will praise thee; for I am
fearfully and wonderfully made"* (Ps. 139:14).

Healing Prayer: Dear heavenly Father, I
believe your Word, which tells me that I am
fearfully and wonderfully made.[1] I am one of
your works, and your works are marvelous. I
thank you that my substance was not hid
from you when you made me in secret. Your
eyes did see my unformed substance, and in
your book all my members were written as
you fashioned me with your hands.[2] Thank
you for these precious truths, dear Father.

Thank you for your everlasting love,
which I experience now, as I pray. Your love,
dear God, helps me to realize there is no condemnation to me because I am in Christ Jesus.
Because I am in Christ, I purpose to walk
according to the Spirit and not according to
the flesh.[3] Thank you for your promise which
assures me that nothing can ever separate me
from your love.[4]

Help me to grow in the grace and
knowledge of Jesus Christ,[5] because I know

that such spiritual growth will help me to see myself as you see me, Father — complete in Jesus Christ.[6] Thank you for creating me in your image.[7] Thank you for Jesus who died for me and set me free from all negative powers.

When I became a Christian, Father, I became a completely new creation in Christ Jesus. In fact, you transformed me into a wonderful, new creation of your own handiwork. The old things are behind me now, and you have made all things new in my life.[8] It thrills me, Father, to realize that you have fully delivered me from the power of darkness, and you have translated me into the kingdom of the Son of your Love, Jesus Christ, my Lord.[9]

Thank you, Father, that you have made me complete in Christ Jesus, and I have put off the old man (including the negative way I used to view myself), and I have put on the new man which is renewed in knowledge after the image of Jesus.[10] Thank you for changing me and helping me to love myself as you love me.

Now, Father, it is my heart-felt desire to stand perfect and complete in your will.[11] Thank you for the truth that helps me to understand that your strength is made perfect in my weakness,[12] and that I do not have to make myself perfect, but you, O God, are perfecting me. Hallelujah!

Thank you, Father, that through Christ I am one of your beloved children.[13] You have made me your child, an heir, and a joint-heir with Christ my Savior.[14] What an amazing truth this is and what a wonderful Father you are. In the name of Jesus I pray, Amen.[15]

References: (1) Psalms 139:14; (2) Psalms 139:15-16; (3) Romans 8:1; (4) Romans 8:38-39; (5) 2 Peter 3:18; (6) Colossians 2:10; (7) Genesis 1:26; (8) 2 Corinthians 5:17; (9) Colossians 1:13; (10) Colossians 3:10; (11) Colossians 4:12; (12) 2 Corinthians 12:9; (13) Ephesians 1:6; (14) Romans 8:17; (15) John 16:23.

77

Nervous Breakdown

*A Healing Prayer to Use if You've
Suffered From a Nervous Breakdown*

Healing Promise: *"For God has not given us a
spirit of fear, but of power and of love and of a
sound mind"* (2 Tim. 1:7, NKJV).

Healing Prayer: O God, my Father, as I come
to you now in the blessed name of Jesus, I
thank you for bringing me through the recent
circumstances and experiences of my life. I
claim your promise that you have not given
me a spirit of fear, but of power and of love
and of a sound mind.[1]

I ask you to heal me of the effects of the
nervous breakdown I experienced and to
renew my mind through the washing of the
water of your Word.[2]

Because of your mercies, mighty Father, I
present my body (and my mind and
emotions) as a living sacrifice to you. I pledge
to you that I will no longer be conformed to
this world, because I know you are transform-
ing me by the renewing of my mind so that I
will be able to prove your good, acceptable,
and perfect will.[3] Thank you, Father.

In your Word you tell me that you wish above all things for me to prosper and to be in health.[4] I ask you to completely heal me now, and I receive your healing touch, as I pray.[5]

Fill me with the Holy Spirit,[6] Father, so I will be able to produce the fruit of the Spirit in all that I do.[7] Lead me by your Spirit, Lord God.[8] How I thank you that I did not receive the spirit of bondage again to fear, but I have received your Spirit of adoption which makes me cry out, "Abba, Father."[9]

I know, dear God, that the sufferings I've gone through are not worthy to be compared with the glory you are going to reveal in me.[10] Therefore, I rejoice, Lord God, that you are working in me both to will and to do of your good pleasure.[11]

Because I know you are for me, Father, I know that nothing can be successful against me.[12] Thank you for the assurance that nothing shall be able to separate me from your healing love — not death nor life, angels nor principalities, things present nor things to come.[13] In all things I am more than a conqueror through Jesus Christ my Lord.[14]

Thank you for healing me, dear Father, and for giving me a peace that surpasses all understanding.[15] I will let your peace rule in

my heart and mind.[16] In Jesus' matchless name
I pray, Amen.[17]

References: *(1) 2 Timothy 1:7; (2) Ephesians 5:26; (3)
Romans 12:1-2; (4) 3 John 2; (5) Mark 11:24; (6)
Ephesians 5:18; (7) Galatians 5:22-23; (8) Romans 8:14;
(9) Romans 8:15; (10) Romans 8:18; (11) Philippians 2:13;
(12) Romans 8:31; (13) Romans 8:38-39; (14) Romans
8:37; (15) Philippians 4:7; (16) Colossians 3:15; (17) John
15:16.*

78

Perfectionism

*A Healing Prayer to Use if You
Struggle With Perfectionism*

Healing Promise: *"Without Me you can do nothing"* (John 15:5, NKJV).

Healing Prayer: Heavenly Father, heal me of perfectionism, and help me to abide in Jesus, that I may bear much fruit.[1] Sometimes I drive myself to distraction with my desire to be perfect. Thank you for showing me that all I am, have, and am able to accomplish comes from you.[2] Keep reminding me that it is in you I live and move and have my being.[3]

Father, nowhere in your Word do you tell me that you have unrealistic expectations of me or require me to be a totally perfect person. Rather you tell me that my expectations are to be in you and my soul is to wait upon you.[4] That is very freeing to me, Father.

Deliver me from perfectionism.[5] Through your grace, dear Father, I have been made a new creation. The old things that have always driven me to perfectionism are truly passed away, and you have made all things new in my life.[6]

I am crucified with Christ. It is no longer I who live, but Christ lives in me, and the life which I now live in the flesh I live by faith in your Son, who loved me and gave himself for me.[7]

In Christ I am complete.[8] Fill me with the knowledge of your will in all wisdom and spiritual understanding so I can walk worthy of you, Lord God, and be fruitful in every good work, as I increase in my knowledge of you.[9]

Father, you are my light and my salvation, and you are the strength of my life.[10] I place all my trust in you, Lord God, and I know that you will direct my paths.[11] Thank you for delivering me from the power of darkness and translating me into the kingdom of the Son of your love, in whom I have redemption through His blood.[12]

How I praise you, mighty Father, that I do not have to make myself perfect, but you are working in me both to will and to do of your good pleasure.[13] I know that you will perfect that which concerns me, and, therefore, I don't have to try to do it all myself.[14] Therefore, I believe and trust you to complete the work you've begun in my life.[15]

Thank you for the Holy Spirit, who empowers me to accomplish great things.[16] Having begun in the Spirit, Father, I renounce any attempt to make myself perfect through the flesh.[17]

Your strength is made perfect in my weakness, and your grace is sufficient for me.[18] Thank you for healing me and delivering me from perfectionism, dear Father. In Jesus' wonderful name I pray, Amen.[19]

References: (1) John 15:5; (2) 2 Peter 1:3; (3) Acts 17:28; (4) Psalms 62:5; (5) Joel 2:32; (6) 2 Corinthians 5:17; (7) Galatians 2:20; (8) Colossians 2:10; (9) Colossians 1:9-10; (10) Psalms 27:1; (11) Proverbs 3:5-6; (12) Colossians 1:13; (13) Philippians 2:13; (14) Psalms 138:8; (15) Philippians 1:6; (16) 1 Corinthians 2:4-5; (17) Galatians 3:3; (18) 2 Corinthians 12:9; (19) John 16:23.

79

Phobias

*A Healing Prayer to Use When
You Suffer From Phobias*

Healing Promise: *"Do not be afraid, nor be dismayed, for the Lord your God is with you wherever you go"* (Josh. 1:9, NKJV).

Healing Prayer: Heavenly Father, thank you for going with me and being with me everywhere.[1] Help me to remember this when phobias, irrational fears, and other anxieties threaten to dismay me. You are my light and my salvation, and, because this is true, there is nothing and no one that I should fear.[2]

Heal me of the phobia that causes me to fear _____.
I receive your healing, Father, and I will no longer be afraid of sudden fear or any other kind of phobia, because you, Lord God, are my confidence, and I know you will keep me safe at all times.[3] Thank you, Father.

I believe you are presently delivering me from all phobias.[4] Help me to walk in your peace, as I keep my mind stayed on you and trust you.[5] You have given great peace to me; therefore, I will not let my heart be troubled or afraid any longer.[6]

Thank you, Father, that I have not received the spirit of bondage to fear. Instead, I have received the Spirit of adoption that causes me to cry, "Abba, Father." Thank you for adopting me into your family.[7]

Father, I know you are my Helper; therefore, I will never fear what people or circumstances can do to me.[8] It's such a wonderful realization to know that there is absolutely no fear in your love. In fact, I rejoice in the certainty that your perfect love is casting out all fear from my life.[9]

Thank you, Father, for delivering me from all phobias and the torments of fear. You have not given me a spirit of fear, but you have given me a spirit of power, of love, and of a sound mind.[10] Fill me with your love, Father. It gives me great joy to believe and receive your love now, as I pray in the wonderful name of Jesus.[11]

Your love is poured forth into my heart by the Holy Spirit whom you have given unto me.[12] I receive your love, and thank you for the power of the Holy Spirit in my life.

Thank you for giving your angels charge over me, to keep me in all my ways.[13] I rejoice in their protection, and in the certainty that you have delivered me from all my phobias and fears.[14] You, O God, have delivered me from all the power of darkness and have translated me into the kingdom of your dear Son, Jesus Christ.[15]

I have been redeemed from the power of all phobias through the blood of Jesus, my Lord.[16] How I praise you, dear God. In the all-powerful name of Jesus I pray, Amen.[17]

References: (1) Joshua 1:9; (2) Psalms 27:1; (3) Proverbs 3:25-26; (4) Psalms 34:4; (5) Isaiah 26:3; (6) John 14:27; (7) Romans 8:15-16; (8) Hebrews 13:6; (9) 1 John 4:18; (10) 2 Timothy 1:7; (11) John 16:24; (12) Romans 5:5; (13) Psalms 91:11; (14) Psalms 34:4; (15) Colossians 1:13; (16) Colossians 1:14; (17) John 15:16.

80

Rejection

*A Healing Prayer to Use When
You Are Feeling Rejected*

Healing Promise: *"He that despiseth you
despiseth me* [Jesus]; *and he that despiseth me
despiseth him that sent me* [God the Father]"
(Luke 10:16).

Healing Prayer: Heavenly Father, thank you
for showing me how to deal with rejection by
sending your Son, who was despised and
rejected of men.[1] It gives me strength and
courage to realize that when others reject me,
I am experiencing some of what Jesus did,
and sometimes it is you and your Son in me
that they actually are rejecting.[2] This helps me
to know that you understand my feelings
completely.[3] Simply knowing this brings a
measure of healing to me already.

The feelings of rejection I have experienced as a result of _____
do cause me hurt and anguish, but I know it is
your will to heal me of these things. Teach me
your will and your way in all things, Lord
God, and lead me in a plain path because of
my enemies.[4] I will continue to seek your face,
because I know that, when others forsake me,
you will take care of me.[5] Thank you, Father.

Because I know this is true, I now cast the cares and pain of rejection over on you, Father, for I know that you care for me.[6] Thank you for healing my feelings, bearing my griefs, and taking my sorrows away through Jesus, my Savior.[7]

You are my helper, mighty God. Therefore, I will not fear what others might do to me. Jesus is my Savior, and He is the same yesterday, today, and forever.[8] He knows and understands what rejection feels like, for He was betrayed,[9] forsaken,[10] mocked, scorned, and persecuted.[11]

Jesus, I thank you for being my faithful friend. I rejoice to know that you will never leave me nor forsake me.[12] Thank you for being a friend who sticks closer than a brother.[13] Lord, I can indeed do all things through you, including facing rejection and persecution without fear.[14] Thank you, Jesus.

Father God, I rejoice in your love for me and I thank you for healing me of the pain of rejection. In the wonderful name of Jesus I pray, Amen.[15]

References: *(1) Isaiah 53:3; (2) Luke 10:16: (3) Hebrews 4:15; (4) Psalms 27:11; (5) Psalms 27:9-10; (6) 1 Peter 5:7; (7) Isaiah 53:4; (8) Hebrews 13:5-8; (9) Mark 14:44; (10) Mark 14:50; (11) Mark 15:16-20; (12) Hebrews 13:5-8; (13) Proverbs 18:24; (14) Philippians 4:13; (15) John 16:23.*

81

Worry

A Healing Prayer to Use When
You Are Worried

Healing Promise: *"Cast thy burden upon the Lord, and he shall sustain thee"* (Ps. 55:22).

Healing Prayer: Thank you, Father, for the healing promise from your Word which tells me to cast my burdens upon you, realizing that you will sustain me.[1] I do so now in the name of Jesus.[2] As I pour out my heart before you, Father, I realize afresh that you alone are my refuge from worry.[3] Thank you, Father.

Therefore, being anxious about nothing, I will let my requests be made known unto you in everything through prayer and supplication. As I do this, the wonderful peace you've provided for me — a peace that surpasses my ability to understand — is truly keeping my heart and mind through Christ Jesus.[4] How wonderful this is to me, Father.

Father, I rejoice in the certainty of your promise to keep me in perfect peace, as I keep my mind stayed upon you and trust fully in you.[5] With your help, I will do this each step of my way. Help me to dwell in your secret place, Father, and to abide under your shadow. You truly are my refuge and my fortress. You are my God, and I will trust in you instead of worrying.[6]

Through your grace I take my stand upon the promise of Jesus who said, "Peace I leave with you, my peace I give unto you. Not as the world gives do I give unto you. Therefore, do not let your heart be troubled or afraid."[7] Thank you, Father. I realize more fully than ever that worry is a form of fear, and I believe with all my heart that your perfect love has cast out all fear from my life.[8] Thank you, Father.

In light of these marvelous discoveries from your Word, I humble myself under your mighty hand and place all my trust in you, Father. Because I know that you will always take care of me, I choose to stop worrying and to trust you completely.

Therefore, I now cast all my cares, fears, and worries upon you, Father, because I know you care for me and you always take good care of me.[9] Thank you for your Word which is a lamp unto my feet and a light unto my path.[10] Thank you, Father, for setting me free from worry. In Jesus' glorious name I pray, Amen.[11]

References: (1) Psalms 55:22; (2) John 16:24; (3) Psalms 62:8; (4) Philippians 4:6-7; (5) Isaiah 26:3; (6) Psalms 91:1-2; (7) John 14:27; (8) 1 John 4:18; (9) 1 Peter 5:7; (10) Psalms 119:105; (11) John 15:16.

Healing

For

Your

Mind

A s we live our lives our minds become conditioned to view God, the world, other people, and ourselves in certain specific ways. Often, our mental conditioning leads us into realms of confusion, doubt, fear, and mistrust — a far cry from what God, our heavenly Father, wants from and for us.

Proverbs tells us that we are profoundly affected by what we think in our hearts. (See Proverbs 23:7.) As we live our lives, our thinking is impacted by the teaching we receive, observations we make, personal experiences, people around us, and other influences, some of which are good and some of which are unhealthy for us. Some of these are consistent with the truth of God's Word and some are not. Sometimes these influences are known at the conscious level, but often the effect upon our thinking is held deeper, at the subconscious level of our being.

These thoughts and influences affect our attitudes, reactions, and behaviors, and they may hinder our spiritual life, until they are recognized and dealt with through the Word of God and the guidance of the Holy Spirit in His ministry of healing and sanctification.

The prayers in this section of *Healing Prayers* are built directly from the Word of God to help you renew your mind according to the Scriptures. As you pray these Scripture prayers, you will discover your thoughts increasingly lining up with God's thoughts, as they are revealed in His Word. This process will bring healing and wholeness to your mind.

Whether your problem is doubt, confusion, double-mindedness, stress, evil thoughts, mental disturbances, or depression, you will find that these prayers will change your mental perspective in many healing ways. The Bible makes it clear that God wants you to have a sound mind at all times.

God promises, "For God has not given us a spirit of fear, but of power and of love and of a sound mind" (2 Tim. 1:7, NKJV). The prayers of this section will deliver you from fear, and enable you to experience God's healing power and love. These dynamic forces, coupled with your faith in God, will help you to experience full soundness of mind — God's wonderful will for you.

"Therefore gird up the loins of your mind, be sober, and rest your hope fully upon the grace that is to be brought to you at the revelation of Jesus Christ" (1 Pet. 1:13, NKJV).

As you pray, remember that God loves you, and He hears and answers your prayers.

82

Confusion

A Healing Prayer for Freedom
From Confusion

Healing Promise: *"For God is not the author of confusion but of peace, as in all the churches of the saints"* (1 Cor. 14:33, NKJV).

Healing Prayer: Almighty Father, how I thank you and praise you that you are not the author of the confusion I am experiencing. I believe you are the author of peace in my life, and I ask you to remove all confusion from my mind.[1] Your Word assures me that when I call unto you, you will answer me and show me great and mighty things that I do not know.[2] Thank you, Father.

Father, thank you, also, for giving me a spirit of power, love, and a sound mind.[3] I claim your promises now, as I pray. I love your Word, Father, and I believe your promise of peace, which is available to all who love your law. Thank you for your Word which enables me to rise above all confusion.[4]

Father, help me always to avoid all envy and strife, for they result in confusion and every evil work.[5] Therefore, I will seek peace and pursue it.[6] To the extent that it depends on me, I will endeavor to live peaceably with all others.[7]

Father, help me to trust in you with all my heart, and not to lean unto my own understanding. In all my ways I will acknowledge you, and I know you will direct my paths.[8] As I cast my burden of confusion upon you, I know you will sustain me.[9] Thank you, Father.

Instead of worrying, Father, I will let my requests be made known unto you. In every thing by prayer and supplication with thanksgiving, I will pray to you. Remove all confusion from my mind. How I praise you, dear Father, for the peace you are imparting to me. Truly, it does surpass all understanding, and it will keep my heart and mind free from all confusion through Christ Jesus.[10] Hallelujah! Thank you for your wonderful peace, Father.

Give me your power, mighty God, and increase your strength in me.[11] I can do all things through Christ who strengthens me.[12] I rejoice in your answers to my prayer, and I thank you that you are supplying all of my needs according to your riches in glory through Christ Jesus.[13] In the matchless name of Jesus I pray, Amen.[14]

References: (1) 1 Corinthians 14:33; (2) Jeremiah 33:3; (3) 2 Timothy 1:7; (4) Psalms 119:165; (5) James 3:16; (6) Psalms 34:14; (7) Romans 12:18; (8) Proverbs 3:5-6; (9)

Psalms 55:22; (10) Philippians 4:6-7; (11) Isaiah 40:29; (12) Philippians 4:13; (13) Philippians 4:19; (14) John 16:23.

83

Conquering the Thought Life

*A Healing Prayer to Enable You
to Master Your Thoughts*

Healing Promise: *"And be not conformed to this world: but be ye transformed by the renewing of your mind, that ye may prove what is that good, and acceptable, and perfect, will of God"* (Rom. 12:2).

Healing Prayer: Mighty God, I do not want to be conformed to this world. Therefore, I ask you to transform me, as I endeavor to renew my mind, so that I will be able to prove your good, acceptable, and perfect will in my life.[1] Through your grace, Father, I will keep my mind stayed on you, and I will trust in you. As I do so, I will always experience your perfect peace in my life.[2] Thank you for your peace.

Always keep me from walking according to my flesh, Father, for I realize that the weapons of spiritual warfare are not carnal, but they are mighty in you for the pulling down of strongholds. Realizing this, I will cast down all arguments and every high thing that exalts itself against knowing you, and I will bring each and every thought into captivity to the obedience of Christ.[3] Help me to do this effectively at all times, Father.

I want to be always spiritually minded, Lord God, because I know that carnal-mindedness brings death, but spiritual-mindedness gives me life and peace.[4] I want the mind of Christ to govern my life and my actions at all times.[5] I choose to set my affection on things above, not on things of the earth.[6] Help me to remember always to think only on things that are true, honest, just, pure, lovely, and of good report.[7]

Father, help me to renew my mind by the washing of the water of your Word.[8] Thank you for giving me the spirit of a sound mind, Father—a sound mind that is filled with power and love, not fear.[9] Thank you for helping me to conquer my thought life and for helping me in every way. Because of your help, I will never again be confounded. I have set my face like a flint, and I know that I shall never be ashamed.[10] In the wonderful name of Jesus I pray, Amen.[11]

References: (1) Romans 12:2; (2) Isaiah 26:3; (3) 2 Corinthians 10:3-5; (4) Romans 8:6; (5) Philippians 2:5; (6) Colossians 3:2; (7) Philippians 4:8; (8) Ephesians 5:26; (9) 2 Timothy 1:7; (10) Isaiah 50:7; (11) John 15:16.

84

Contentment

A Prayer for Greater Contentment
in Your Life

Healing Promise: *"Godliness with contentment is great gain"* (1 Tim. 6:6).

Healing Prayer: Mighty Father, I believe the truth of your Word, which proclaims that godliness with contentment is great gain for me.[1] Thank you for giving such "great gain" to me, dear God. Feed me with food that is needful and convenient for me, as I endeavor to walk in contentment from this time forward.[2] Thank you for giving me peace with you, Father, through my Lord Jesus Christ.[3]

You have imparted your peace to me, and I have discovered that it truly is a peace that surpasses all understanding.[4] Thank you, Father. I greatly rejoice that you will teach how to be content in whatever state I find myself.[5]

It is my desire to be content at all times, Father. Help me to be content with whatever I have.[6] Having all of my needs supplied according to your riches in glory[7] leads me to be content with the things you've provided for me each day.[8] Thank you, Father.

Father God, help me to quiet myself so that my soul may be steady and calm.[9] I know that in quietness and confidence shall be my strength.[10] Therefore, I will be still to hear your voice[11] and know that you are God.[12]

Bless me, Father, and keep me. Make your face to shine upon me, and be gracious unto me. Lift up your countenance upon me, and give me your peace.[13] Your blessing in my life makes me content, and my sense of contentment helps me realize your promise that goodness and mercy shall follow me all the days of my life, and I will dwell in your house forever.[14] Thank you, Father. In Jesus' name I pray, Amen.[15]

References: (1) 1 Timothy 6:6; (2) Proverbs 30:8; (3) Romans 5:1; (4) Philippians 4:7; (5) Philippians 4:11; (6) Hebrews 13:5; (7) Philippians 4:19; (8) 1 Timothy 6:8; (9) Psalms 131:2; (10) Isaiah 30:15; (11) 1 Kings 19:12; (12) Psalms 46:10; (13) Numbers 6:24-26; (14) Psalms 23:6; (15) John 16:23.

85

Double-Mindedness

A Healing Prayer for Freedom
From Double-Mindedness

Healing Promise: *"If any of you lacks wisdom, let him ask of God, who gives to all liberally and without reproach, and it will be given him. But let him ask in faith, with no doubting, for he who doubts is like a wave of the sea driven and tossed by the wind"* (James 1:5-6, NKJV).

Healing Prayer: Heavenly Father, I ask you for your wisdom to help me find complete freedom from all double-mindedness in my life. Thank you for giving so liberally to me when I ask in faith, without doubting.[1] I do so now, Father, fully realizing that my double-mindedness has prevented me from receiving from your hands.[2] Whenever I am double-minded I become unstable in all my ways.[3]

Forgive me for thinking at variance with your Word, Father, and for any other form of double-mindedness. I thank you for your promise to forgive me and to cleanse me from all unrighteousness, when I confess my sins to you.[4] I believe this truth of your Word, Father, and I receive your forgiveness and cleansing now, as I pray.

I realize that double-mindedness is having two opinions about the same subject and shifting back and forth from one opinion to the other. It does me no good to trust your Word and then to turn around and doubt your Word. Therefore, Father, I purpose in my heart and set my face like flint[5] to trust you and your Word. I know that you are not a man and you do not lie,[6] indeed it is impossible for you to lie.[7]

Father God, your way is perfect, and your Word is tried. Thank you for being a buckler to me as I place my trust in you.[8] I realize double-mindedness stems from doubt, so I will pray and believe your Word, because I know that faith comes by hearing, and hearing by your Word.[9]

Father, I reaffirm that your Word will never return unto you void, but it will accomplish that which you please and it will always prosper in the things for which you send it.[10] Thank you, mighty God.

How grateful I am that you've made it possible for me to be of good courage, as you strengthen my heart. I hope in you, Lord God.[11] You are on my side. Therefore, I will not fear anything.[12] Rather, I will place my faith and hope in you, Father; and I will not cast my confidence away by being double-minded any longer. Thank you for your promise to reward me, as I diligently seek you.[13]

All these things I pray in the mighty name of Jesus, Amen.[14]

References: *(1) James 1:5-6; (2) James 1:7; (3) James 1:8; (4) 1 John 1:9; (5) Isaiah 50:7; (6) Numbers 23:19; (7) Hebrews 6:18; (8) Psalms 18:30; (9) Romans 10:17; (10) Isaiah 55:11; (11) Psalms 31:24; (12) Psalms 118:6; (13) Hebrews 10:35; (14) John 15:16.*

86

Doubt

*A Healing Prayer to Use When
Struggling With Doubt*

Healing Promise: *"So then faith cometh by hearing, and hearing by the word of God"* (Rom. 10:17).

Healing Prayer: Father in heaven, there are times when I struggle with doubt in my life. Help me, I pray, to overcome unbelief in my life at all times.[1] I want to be a person of great faith, so I ask you to help me remember at all times that nothing is too hard for you, Lord God.[2]

I will place my trust in you all the time.[3] As I pour out my heart before you, Father, I realize that you truly are my refuge.[4] All my strength is in you.[5] As I put my unswerving trust in you, it is then that I know I am safe.[6] You are my salvation, Lord God; I will trust in you, and not be afraid.[7] Instead of being filled with fear, I will continue to believe your Word.[8]

Thank you for the wonderful prayer promises you've given to me, such as your promise that I will receive the things I desire when I pray, as long as I truly believe.[9] I want to be a believer who is full of faith, not doubt, dear Father.

Lord God, I believe that all things work together for good in my life, because I love you and I know you have called me according to your purposes.[10] Help me to remember that whatever is not of faith is sin.[11] Assist me in standing fast in the faith you've imparted to me.[12]

Through your grace, Father, I will walk by faith and not by sight from now on.[13] Help me to hold tightly to the shield of faith with which I will be able to quench all the fiery darts of doubt that come my way.[14]

Help me to hold fast the profession of my faith without wavering,[15] because I realize that without faith it is impossible to please you, Father.[16] I will feed upon your Word daily and receive the faith that comes as I hear your words.[17]

When the enemy comes to sow thoughts of doubt and unbelief, I will obey your Word and bring those thoughts captive unto the obedience of Christ.[18] I will resist the devil and I will stand against him steadfast in the faith.[19]

I dedicate myself to being strong in faith, giving all the glory to you, Father, for I am fully persuaded that what you have promised you are also able to perform.[20] Therefore, I will not be double-minded, wanting to believe, but wavering. Rather, I will be stable in all my ways, strong in faith, and thus, able to receive the wonderful blessings you have for me.[21] I will resist all doubt from the enemy, and it must flee from me.[22] Hallelujah!

These things I pray and believe, in Jesus' wonderful name.[23] Amen.

References: *(1) Mark 9:24; (2) Genesis 18:14; (3) Psalms 62:8; (4) Psalms 62:8; (5) Psalms 84:5; (6) Proverbs 29:25; (7) Isaiah 12:2; (8) Matthew 8:26; (9) Mark 11:24; (10) Romans 8:28; (11) Romans 14:23; (12) 1 Corinthians 16:13; (13) 2 Corinthians 5:7; (14) Ephesians 6:16; (15) Hebrews 10:23; (16) Hebrews 11:6; (17) Romans 10:17; (18) 2 Corinthians 10:4-5; (19) 1 Peter 5:9; (20) Romans 4:20-21; (21) James 1:6-8; (22) James 4:7; (23) John 16:23.*

87

Establishing Your Thoughts

A Healing Prayer to Help You
Establish Your Thoughts

Healing Promise: *"Be anxious for nothing, but in everything by prayer and supplication, with thanksgiving, let your requests be made known to God; and the peace of God, which surpasses all understanding, will guard your hearts and minds through Christ Jesus"* (Phil. 4:6-7, NKJV).

Healing Prayer: Heavenly Father, I thank you for your Word, which is a lamp unto my feet and a light unto my path.[1] Enable me to walk in the light of your Word at all times. As I do so, I realize that I will never have to worry again. Instead, through prayer and supplication with thanksgiving, I will let my requests be made known unto you. Thank you for your wonderful promise to let your peace, which surpasses all understanding, keep my heart and mind through Christ Jesus.[2] I claim that promise for my thought life now, Father.

Thank you for bringing me up out of the horrible pit in which I found myself, out of the miry clay, and for setting my feet upon the solid rock of your Word.[3] In so doing, Father, you have helped me establish my thoughts. Indeed, I have discovered that you are my refuge and strength, a very present help to me in times of trouble.[4] Thank you, Father.

I rejoice in your great faithfulness to me, Father, for I know that you are establishing me, and you are keeping me from all evil.[5] Thank you, mighty God. Help me to walk worthy of you, unto all pleasing. Help me to be fruitful in every good work. Help me to increase in my knowledge of you.[6]

Strengthen me with all might, according to your glorious power, unto all patience and longsuffering with joyfulness.[7] Eternal God, you are my refuge, and underneath me are your everlasting arms, supporting me.[8] Thank you for establishing my thoughts according to your Word.

God, you are my strength. You are making my feet like hinds' feet and encouraging me to walk upon high places without fear.[9] You are my confidence, Father, and I know you will help me to keep my footing.[10] Thank you for giving me perfect peace, as I keep my mind stayed upon you and continue to trust in you.[11] In Jesus' name I pray, Amen.[12]

References: (1) Psalms 119:105; (2) Philippians 4:6-7; (3) Psalms 40:2; (4) Psalms 46:1; (5) 2 Thessalonians 3:3; (6) Colossians 1:10; (7) Colossians 1:11; (8) Deuteronomy 33:27; (9) Habakkuk 3:19; (10) Proverbs 3:26; (11) Isaiah 26:3; (12) John 15:16.

88

Evil Thoughts

*A Healing Prayer for Victory
Over Evil Thoughts*

Healing Promise: *"For my thoughts are not your thoughts, neither are your ways my ways, saith the Lord. For as the heavens are higher than the earth, so are my ways higher than your ways, and my thoughts than your thoughts"* (Isa. 55:8-9).

Healing Prayer: Mighty God, I seek freedom from all evil thoughts. Help me to line up my thoughts with yours, for I realize that there is a wide gap between your thoughts and my thoughts and between your ways and my ways.[1] Father, forgive me for the evil imaginations and thoughts I have entertained in my heart.[2] Help me to control my thought life at all times.

Father, I realize that evil thoughts may be darts from the enemy or may be from my own flesh or even my surroundings. Help me, Father, when such thoughts come, to take my thoughts captive before they can exalt themselves against you and your truth.[3]

Remove all vanity from my thinking, Father.[4] Replace all wrong thinking with the wonderful comfort and peace that comes to me through the Holy Spirit.[5] I hate vain thoughts, Lord God, but I love your Word.[6]

Teach me how to apply my heart to wisdom,[7] and to behold wondrous things from your Word, as I meditate upon it both night and day.[8] Your Word is truth, Father.[9] As I continually abide in your Word, I will know the truth, and your truth will make me free.[10]

Search me, O God, and know my heart; try me, and know my thoughts, and see if there be any wicked way in me and lead me in the way everlasting.[11] I want all of my thoughts to be righteous thoughts, and I want your righteousness to invade and permeate my thoughts and my life.[12] Therefore, I commit my works unto you, Father, knowing that, in so doing, my thoughts will be established.[13] Thank you for showing me that the thoughts of the diligent always lead to abundant living.[14]

Deliver me from evil in all its ugly forms, dear Father, and from evil thoughts in particular.[15] Thank you for hearing and answering my prayer. In Jesus' glorious name I pray, Amen.[16]

References: (1) Isaiah 55:8-9; (2) Genesis 6:5; (3) 2 Corinthians 10:5; (4) Psalms 94:11; (5) John 14:26; (6) Psalms 119:113; (7) Psalms 90:12; (8) Psalms 1:2; (9) John 17:17; (10) John 8:32; (11) Psalms 139:23-24; (12) Proverbs 12:5; (13) Proverbs 16:3; (14) Proverbs 21:5; (15) Matthew 6:13; (16) John 16:23.

89

Judgmentalism

A Healing Prayer for Freedom
From Being Judgmental

Healing Promise: *"Beloved, let us love one another, for love is of God; and everyone who loves is born of God and knows God"* (1 John 4:7, NKJV).

Healing Prayer: Heavenly Father, I want to be obedient to Jesus, who admonishes me not to judge others. When I realize that I will be judged in the same way I judge others, I recognize how important it is for me to avoid being judgmental in any way.[1]

As I come to you now, in the name of Jesus Christ, I repent of my critical and judgmental attitudes and I ask you to forgive me and cleanse me of all unrighteousness.[2] I receive your forgiveness and cleansing, and I thank you for your goodness to me.

Thank you, also, for enabling me to walk in freedom from any tendency to be judgmental. With your continued help, I will not judge others. Instead, I will seek to restore others, and, as I do so, I will consider myself, lest I should fall into the same temptation.[3]

Enable me, precious Father, to stand fast in the liberty you've given to me, so I will never again be entangled with a yoke of bondage to being judgmental.[4] Father, help me to walk in love toward all others[5] and to bear the burdens of others, for, in so doing I fulfill the Law of Christ.[6]

Above all things, I want to put on love, which is the bond of perfection and which is the evidence of true Christian maturity,[7] because I realize that, when I love others, I am fulfilling your highest will and I am abiding in the light.[8] I want to abide in your light and love, heavenly Father. I know that abiding in your love is abiding in you, for you are love.[9] As your dear child and with your help, I will follow you and I will walk in love, as Christ also has loved me.[10]

Father, from this time forward, I will avoid being judgmental by accepting and receiving others as you have accepted and received me in Christ Jesus.[11] In Jesus' blessed name I pray, Amen.[12]

References: (1) Matthew 7:1-2; (2) 1 John 1:9; (3) Galatians 6:1; (4) Galatians 5:1; (5) Ephesians 5:2; (6) Galatians 6:2; (7) Colossians 3:14; (8) 1 John 2:10; (9) 1 John 4:7; (10) Ephesians 5:1-2; (11) Romans 15:7; (12) John 15:16.

90

Meditating on God's Word

*A Prayer to Help You Meditate
on the Word of God*

Healing Promise: *"But his delight is in the law of the Lord, and in His law he meditates day and night. He shall be like a tree planted by the rivers of water, that brings forth its fruit in its season, whose leaf also shall not wither; and whatever he does shall prosper"* (Ps. 1:2-3, NKJV).

Healing Prayer: Heavenly Father, thank you for your Word and for all the personal promises it contains, especially your promise of fruitfulness and prosperity to those who meditate upon your Word daily. I claim this promise, as I pray, and I promise you that I will be one of those who reaps your promises of fruitfulness and prosperity as a result of regular Bible mediation.[1]

Help me, Father, to walk not in the counsel of the ungodly. Help me not to stand in the path of sinners or sit in the seat of the scornful.[2] My delight is in your Word, and I will meditate upon its precepts both night and day.[3]

Father, make me strong and courageous to observe and to do according to your Word. Through your grace, I will not turn to the right hand or to the left, and this will lead me into the prosperity you've promised to me.[4]

Father, I commit myself not to let your Word depart from my mouth. I will meditate in it day and night, and this will lead me to do what your Word says. The promised result will be my inheritance — it will make my way prosperous and it will assure my good success.[5] Thank you, Father, for your promise of prosperity and success, which comes from meditating upon your Word.

Father, I will attend to your words and incline my ear to your sayings. I will keep them before my eyes and in the midst of my heart, for they are life to me and health to all my flesh.[6]

Enable me to walk in your statutes and keep your commandments and to do them, as your Word directs.[7] Make your face to shine upon me and be gracious unto me.[8] I will always endeavor to obey and serve you, Father, and I know this will permit me to spend my days in prosperity and my years in pleasures.[9] Thank you, mighty God.

Father, thank you for your promise to make me the head and not the tail and to place me above only and not beneath.[10] I thank you that you establish my thoughts, as I commit my works totally to you.[11]

I love you, Father, and I love your Word. I promise that I will meditate on your precepts and have respect to your ways.[12] I will always delight myself in your statutes and I will not forget thy Word.[13] Thank you for your Word. In the name of Jesus I pray, Amen.[14]

References: (1) Psalms 1:2-3; (2) Psalms 1:1; (3) Psalms 1:2; (4) Joshua 1:7; (5) Joshua 1:8; (6) Proverbs 4:20-22; (7) Leviticus 26:3-4; (8) Numbers 6:25; (9) Job 36:11; (10) Deuteronomy 28:13; (11) Proverbs 16:3; (12) Psalms 119:15; (13) Psalms 119:16; (14) John 16:23.

91

Mental Disorders

*A Healing Prayer to Use if You
Suffer From Mental Disorders*

Healing Promise: *"For God hath not given us the spirit of fear; but of power, and of love, and of a sound mind"* (2 Tim. 1:7).

Healing Prayer: Father, I am convinced it is not your will for me to suffer from this mental disorder any longer. Therefore, I claim your promise of mental soundness, because I believe you have not given me a spirit of fear, but one of power, love, and a sound mind.[1] Thank you, Father.

I will not fear because I know you are with me. I will not be dismayed because I know you are my God. Thank you for strengthening me, helping me, and upholding me with the right hand of your righteousness.[2]

Deliver me, Father, from this mental disorder, and cause me to escape.[3] Incline your ear to me, and save me.[4] Make your mighty power known to me.[5] I cry to you in the midst of my trouble, Father, and I know you are saving me out of all my distresses.[6]

How I thank you that you are not the author of confusion, but you are the God of peace,[7] and I believe this applies to my mental health, dear Father.

Therefore, I will not worry, but in every thing, by prayer and supplication with thanksgiving I will let my requests be made known to you. Thank you, Father, for your related promise that assures me of your peace — a peace that surpasses all understanding — which shall keep my heart and mind through Christ Jesus.[8] I love your Word, and I thank you for the peace it imparts to me.[9]

Bring my soul out of prison, so that I will ever be able to praise your name.[10] Help me to stand fast in the liberty wherewith Christ has set me free, and never again to be entangled with the yoke of bondage to any mental disorder or disability.[11] I commit my life and my works totally to you, Lord God, and I thank you that as I do so, my thoughts shall be established.[12]

I will praise you, O God, for you will help me; therefore, I will not be confounded.[13] I believe your Word, and I now proclaim that by your grace I have the mind of Christ.[14] I bless your name, Lord God, for I know you are working within me both to will and to do of your good pleasure.[15]

Thank you for healing my mind and for giving me complete freedom and peace, dear

Father. In the matchless name of Jesus I pray,
Amen.[16]

*References: (1) 2 Timothy 1:7; (2) Isaiah 41:10; (3)
Psalms 71:2; (4) Psalms 71:2; (5) Psalms 106:8; (6)
Psalms 107:19; (7) 1 Corinthians 14:33; (8) Philippians
4:6-7; (9) Psalms 119:165; (10) Psalms 142:7; (11)
Galatians 5:1; (12) Proverbs 16:3; (13) Isaiah 50:7; (14) 1
Corinthians 2:16; (15) Philippians 2:13; (16) John 15:16.*

92

Mental Strongholds

A Healing Prayer to Use in
Demolishing Mental Strongholds

Healing Promise: *"Whosoever shall call on the name of the Lord shall be delivered"* (Joel 2:32).

Healing Prayer: Heavenly Father, certain mental strongholds have prevented me from moving on with you. I ask you to overthrow these strongholds in the name of Jesus. Specifically, I ask you to conquer the stronghold of _____ in my life.

Though I walk in the flesh, dear Father, I realize that I do not war according to the flesh.[1] Therefore, I call upon you to deliver me from the strongholds that threaten to undo me.[2] Thank you for giving me the spiritual weapons of your Word,[3] the name of Jesus,[4] the blood of Jesus,[5] and the word of my testimony[6] to conquer all forces of evil in my life.

I raise these weapons now in the name of Jesus Christ, Father, and I ask you, in the name of Jesus, that the full blessings, power, and merits of the precious blood of Jesus will have full force and effect to destroy and cleanse me from any mental strongholds in my life that would in any way hinder my walk with you.

Thank you for showing me that my weapons are not carnal, but they are mighty in you for the pulling down of this stronghold.[7] Through your power, Almighty God, I cast down all arguments and every high thing that exalts itself against knowing you, and I bring every one of my thoughts into captivity to the obedience of Christ.[8]

Continue your work of deliverance in my life,[9] and help me to stand fast in the liberty you've given to me.[10] I put on all the armor you've given to me, Father, so that I will be able to stand against the wiles of the devil.[11] I take the shield of faith which I will use to quench all the fiery darts of the wicked one,[12] and I will wear the helmet of salvation to protect my mind at all times.[13] Help me always to wield the sword of your Spirit, which is your mighty Word,[14] and to pray always with all prayer and supplication in the Spirit.[15]

Now that I've sought you and I know you've heard me, I realize that you have delivered me from the strongholds that have held me back so long.[16] From this day forward I will be strong in you, Lord God, and in the power of your might.[17] Thank you so much, O God. In Jesus' wonderful name I pray, Amen.[18]

References: *(1) 2 Corinthians 10:3; (2) Psalms 71:2; (3) Hebrews 4:12; (4) Philippians 2:9-10; (5) Revelation 12:11; (6) Revelation 12:11; (7) 2 Corinthians 10:4; (8) 2 Corinthians 10:5; (9) Psalms 91:15; (10) Galatians 5:1; (11) Ephesians 6:11; (12) Ephesians 6:16; (13) Ephesians 6:17; (14) Ephesians 6:17; (15) Ephesians 6:18; (16) Daniel 6:27; (17) Ephesians 6:10; (18) John 16:23.*

93

The Mind of Christ

A Healing Prayer to Let the
Mind of Christ Be in You

Healing Promise: *"Let this mind be in you which was also in Christ Jesus, who, being in the form of God, did not consider it robbery to be equal with God, but made Himself of no reputation, taking the form of a bondservant, and coming in the likeness of men"* (Phil. 2:5-6, NKJV).

Healing Prayer: Dear God, help me to have the mind of Christ.[1] He came to this earth as a servant, and I want to serve you and others in the humility of Jesus.[2] I want to follow His example at all times, Father.[3]

Therefore, I ask you to fill me afresh daily with the Holy Spirit,[4] so I will be able to produce His fruit in all the relationships and responsibilities of my life.[5] As the Holy Spirit teaches me, I will learn more fully what it means to have the mind of Christ.[6] Thank you for His faithfulness in my life, dear Father.

How I praise you for the Holy Spirit who reveals to me all the wonderful things you've freely given to me,[7] including the mind of Christ.[8] As Christ Jesus did, I want to set all my affections on things above, not on things of this earth.[9] Help me, Father, to think on things that are true, honest, just, pure, lovely and of good report, because I know from your Word that these are the kinds of thoughts Jesus thinks.[10]

Father, I purpose in my heart to abide in Christ at all times, because I know this will enable me to be fruitful and to walk as He walked.[11] I will do these things, Lord God, looking unto Jesus, who is the Author and Finisher of my faith, who for the joy that was set before Him endured the cross, despising the shame, and is now sitting with you in the Kingdom of heaven.[12]

Thank you for allowing me to be a friend of Jesus, and, as His friend, I am learning more and more about you and your ways, Father. In fact, Jesus is revealing things to me that you have revealed to Him.[13] I treasure this knowledge He is imparting to me, dear God, and I thank you for allowing the mind of Christ to be in me.

Because of these truths, which I do believe, Father, and your wonderful grace, which I have received, I now proclaim that I have the mind of Christ.[14] In the mighty name of Jesus I pray, Amen.[15]

References: (1) Philippians 2:5-6; (2) Philippians 2:8; (3) 1 Peter 2:21; (4) Ephesians 5:18; (5) Galatians 5:22-23; (6) John 14:26; (7) 1 Corinthians 2:12; (8) 1 Corinthians 2:16;

*(9) Colossians 3:2; (10) Philippians 4:8; (11) John 15:4;
(12) Hebrews 12:2; (13) John 15:15; (14) 2 Corinthians
2:16; (15) John 15:16.*

94

Peace of Mind

*A Healing Prayer to Enable You
to Experience Peace of Mind*

Healing Promise: *"You will keep him in perfect peace, whose mind is stayed on You, because he trusts in You"* (Isa. 26:3, NKJV).

Healing Prayer: Dear Father, I thank you for your promise to keep me in perfect peace, as I keep my mind stayed on you and trust in you.[1] With your help, I will trust in you with all my heart, leaning not upon my own understanding. In all my ways I will acknowledge you, and I know you will bless me by directing my paths.[2] This certainty gives me great peace of mind, Father. Thank you so much.

You have told me to seek and pursue peace, Father,[3] and this I will do through your grace. I love your truth and peace.[4] Thank you for the peace that Jesus imparts to me.[5] His is a peace that the world cannot give and the world cannot take away.[6] In fact, He is my peace.[7] These truths from your Word, Father, give me great peace of mind. How I thank you for your peace!

Realizing these truths you have shown me, I will let your peace rule in my heart.[8]

Trusting in you, I will not allow myself to be anxious about anything, but in everything, by prayer and supplication, with thanksgiving, I will always let my requests be made known unto you, Father.[9] As I obey you in this, I believe I will always experience your peace — a peace which passes all understanding — and your peace will always guard my heart and mind through Christ Jesus.[10] Thank you, Father.

Therefore, dear God, I will endeavor always to think on things that are true, noble, just, pure, lovely, and of good report.[11] This will enable me to experience peace of mind at all times. I will meditate in your Word, for I know that those who love your Word have great peace, and nothing shall cause them to be offended or stumble.[12]

Thank you for the mental peace you give to me, dear Father. In Jesus name I pray, Amen.[13]

References: *(1) Isaiah 26:3; (2) Proverbs 3:5-6; (3) Psalms 34:14; (4) Zechariah 8:19; (5) John 14:27; (6) John 14:27; (7) Ephesians 2:14; (8) Colossians 3:15; (9) Philippians 4:6; (10) Philippians 4:7; (11) Philippians 4:8; (12) Psalms 119:165; (13) John 16:23.*

95

Renewing Your Mind

A Prayer for Renewing Your Mind

Healing Promise: *"I beseech you therefore, brethren, by the mercies of God, that you present your bodies a living sacrifice, holy, acceptable to God, which is your reasonable service. And do not be conformed to this world, but be transformed by the renewing of your mind, that you may prove what is that good and acceptable and perfect will of God"* (Rom. 12:1-2, NKJV).

Healing Prayer: Mighty Father, I ask you to help me renew my mind, as I present my body as a living sacrifice, holy and acceptable to you. I understand that this is my reasonable service of worship unto you. By your mercies to me I will not be conformed to this world any longer. Instead, I will be transformed by the renewing of my mind, and then I will be able to prove what is your good, acceptable, and perfect will.[1] Thank you for helping me to renew my mind, dear Father.

Thank you for restoring my soul and renewing my mind, Lord God.[2] As I wait upon you, I experience renewal of my mind and my strength.[3] Thank you, Father. Help me to put off, concerning my former conduct, the old nature, which grows corrupt according to deceitful lusts, and help me to be renewed in the spirit of my mind, so that I will be able to put on the new nature, which was created according to your will in true righteousness and holiness.[4]

Sanctify and cleanse me, Father, with the washing of water by your Word,[5] for your Word is a lamp unto my feet and a light unto my path.[6] Father, I thank you for your grace, which leads me into thanksgiving and rejoicing and keeps me from ever losing heart. You are renewing my inner person — and my mind — day by day.[7] From this point forward I will focus, not on the things that are seen, but on the things which are not seen, because I realize (through your glorious Word) that the things which are seen are temporary, but the things that are not seen are eternal.[8]

Help me, Father, to put on the new person, who is renewed in knowledge according to your image.[9] Thank you for renewing my mind. I will show forth that renewal through mercy, kindness, humility, meekness, and longsuffering, as I bear with and forgive others in the same way Christ has forgiven me.[10] Thank you, Father. In the name of Jesus I pray, Amen.[11]

References: (1) Romans 12:1-2; (2) Psalms 23:3; (3) Isaiah 40:31; (4) Ephesians 4:22-24; (5) Ephesians 5:26;

(6) Psalms 119:105; (7) 2 Corinthians 4:16; (8) 2 Corinthians 4:18; (9) Colossians 3:10; (10) Colossians 3:10-13; (11) John 15:16.

96

God's Rest

A Healing Prayer to Enjoy God's Rest

Healing Promise: *"There remaineth therefore a rest to the people of God. For he that is entered into his rest, he also hath ceased from his own works, as God did from his. Let us labour therefore to enter into that rest, lest any man fall after the same example of unbelief"* (Heb. 4:9-11).

Healing Prayer: Heavenly Father, I thank you and praise you for the promise of rest that you have given to me. Keep me from all hardness of heart, unbelief, and disobedience, for those attitudes will always prevent me from finding your wonderful rest.[1] Indeed, with your help, I will strive to find your rest and cease from my own works.[2] Thank you, Father.

Keep me from trying so hard in my own strength that I fail to trust in you. Help me to understand that the real labor of the spiritual life is to enter your rest through faith in you and your Word.[3] Thank you for your gracious invitation to come to you when I am weary and heavy-laden, knowing that you will give me your rest. This I now do, and I take the yoke of Jesus Christ upon me as I learn your ways, realizing that He is my example, He is meek and lowly in heart, and He provides my soul with rest. Thank you, Father, that the yoke of Jesus is easy and His burden is light.[4]

I will bless you, O God, for you have given me counsel. My heart instructs me in the night seasons. I will set you always before me, Father. Because you are at my right hand, I shall not be moved. Therefore, my heart is glad and my glory rejoices in you. This enables my flesh to rest in your hope, dear God.[5] Thank you for showing me the path of life, and for showing me that there is fullness of joy in your presence. At your right hand, dear Father, there are pleasures forevermore.[6]

Already, I am finding my rest in you. I wait patiently before you, now. I trust and delight in you, mighty God, and I commit my way unto you.[7] Thank you for giving me rest in my weariness and bringing a sense of refreshment to my heart.[8] Thank you for being my safe place of refuge and rest.[9]

My heart is still, Father, for I have truly found my rest in you. I know that you are my God, and I thank you for giving me your blessed rest.[10] In the wonderful name of Jesus I pray, Amen.[11]

References: (1) Hebrews 3:6-19; (2) Hebrews 4:9-11; (3) Hebrews 4:1-11; (4) Matthew 11:28-30; (5) Psalms 16:7-9; (6) Psalms 16:11; (7) Psalms 37:4-7; (8) Isaiah 28:12; (9) Psalms 46:11; (10) Psalms 46:10; (11) John 16:23.

97

Stress

*A Healing Prayer to Help
You Overcome Stress*

Healing Promise: *"Casting all your care upon him; for he careth for you"* (1 Pet. 5:7).

Healing Prayer: Heavenly Father, during this stressful time in my life, I feel so fortunate to know that your invitation to cast all my cares upon you is still open to me, because you truly do love me and care for me.[1] Therefore, I cast my burdens and cares upon you now. I let go of them and release them all to you, and I believe you are sustaining me.[2] Thank you, mighty God.

You are my refuge and strength, a very present help to me during this time. Therefore, I will not fear.[3] In fact, your perfect love for me is casting out all fear from my life.[4] Thank you, Father. Thank you for preserving me from all evil, and for preserving my soul. I trust you to preserve my going out and my coming in from this time forth, and even for evermore.[5]

During this season of stress, I will trust in you, dear God. I will praise your Word, for I have put my complete trust in you. Therefore, I will not fear and I will not be anxious any more.[6] As I cry unto you, dear Father, I know that all my enemies are turning back. I know this because I know you are for me.[7] Realizing that you are truly for me, I know that nothing can be against me.[8] Hallelujah!

Help me to see more clearly than I've ever seen before that nothing shall be able to separate me from your love which is in Christ Jesus, my Lord.[9] Thank you for always being with me, O God, and for strengthening me. You are helping me, even as I pray, and I know you are upholding me with the right hand of your righteousness.[10]

I am committed to trust you completely, Father, and not to be worried or anxious about anything. I will make my requests to you, and I know that your peace, which surpasses all understanding, will keep my heart and my mind in Christ Jesus.[11] I will trust in you with all my heart and acknowledge you in all my ways, Father, and I know that you will direct my paths.[12]

Thank you, Father, for helping me to be free of all unhealthy stress. In Jesus' name I pray, Amen.[13]

References: (1) 1 Peter 1:7; (2) Psalms 55:22; (3) Psalms 46:1; (4) 1 John 4:18; (5) Psalms 121:7-8; (6) Psalms 56:3-4; (7) Psalms 56:9; (8) Romans 8:31; (9) Romans 8:38-39; (10) Isaiah 41:10; (11) Philippians 4:6-7; (12) Proverbs 3:5-6; (13) John 15:16.

98

Trusting God

A Prayer to Help You Trust
God With All Your Heart

Healing Promise: *"Trust in the Lord with all your heart, and lean not on your own understanding; in all your ways acknowledge Him, and He shall direct your paths"* (Prov. 3:5-6, NKJV).

Healing Prayer: Healing Father, thank you for all the wonderful promises of your Word. They lead me to trust in you with all my heart and not lean on my own understanding. Help me acknowledge you in all my ways, and keep on leading me and directing my paths.[1] Through your grace, I shall walk in trust from this day forward.

As I put my complete and unswerving trust in you, Father, I rejoice and shout for joy,[2] for you are my rock, my fortress, and my deliverer. You are my God and my strength, and I will always trust in you.[3] Though some may trust in horses and chariots and other personal resources and abilities, I will remember your name, Lord God,[4] and trust in you alone.

Father, you tell me in your Word that as I trust in you, I am assured of dwelling in a good land and being fed. Moreover, as I commit my way to you and trust in you, you will bring to pass the desires you have put in my heart and the life purpose for which I was created.[5] Trusting you is so wonderful, Father.

It gives me great joy and peace to commit my way unto you as I trust in you.[6] Trusting you, Father, puts me in a state of blessedness.[7] Thank you so much for your great love and grace, which make this possible for me. In you, O God, I have placed my trust; therefore, I have no reason to fear.[8] Trusting in you makes me completely happy.[9]

I will trust in you forever, Lord God, for you are my everlasting strength.[10] Thank you for loving me and knowing me, as I place all my trust in you.[11] Take my hand, as I walk in trust minute by minute and day by day. In Jesus' matchless name I pray, Amen.[12]

References: *(1) Proverbs 3:5-6; (2) Psalms 5:11; (3) Psalms 18:2; (4) Psalms 20:7; (5) Psalms 37:3-5; (6) Psalms 37:3-5; (7) Psalms 40:4; (8) Psalms 56:4; (9) Proverbs 16:20; (10) Isaiah 26:4; (11) Nahum 1:7, (12) John 16:23-24.*

99

Wisdom

A Prayer to Receive God's Wisdom

Healing Promise: *"If any of you lacks wisdom, let him ask of God, who gives to all liberally and without reproach, and it will be given to him"* (James 1:5, NKJV).

Healing Prayer: Wonderfully wise Father, I come to you to seek wisdom for my life. Thank you for reminding me that all the treasures of wisdom and knowledge, which are hidden in my Savior, Jesus Christ, are not hidden from me, but for me, as a believer.[1]

As I seek your wisdom, I happily remember that Jesus is made wisdom unto me,[2] and that you are a rewarder of those who diligently seek you.[3]

Thank you for your promise that you want to give wisdom to me liberally and without reproach.[4] I receive your promises of wisdom now, as I pray in faith, nothing wavering.[5] It will be my privilege, Lord God, to partake of and walk in your wisdom from this day forward.

Your wisdom in my life is truly invaluable, Father.[6] Teach me to number my days, that I may always apply my heart to wisdom.[7] You are the Giver of every good and perfect gift, the Father of lights, who does not change.[8]

I reverence you, Father.[9] Thank you for giving your wisdom to me.[10] I listen for the knowledge and understanding which always proceed from your mouth.[11]

Your wisdom gives me great happiness, Lord God.[12] All the things I desire cannot be compared with your matchless wisdom.[13] As I walk in your wisdom, Father, I find pleasantness for my life, and peace.[14] Your wisdom is a tree of life to me.[15] I will not forsake your wisdom, because I know it will preserve me and keep me.[16] Thank you for your wisdom, Father. In the blessed name of Jesus I pray, Amen.[17]

References: (1) Colossians 2:2-3; (2) 1 Corinthians 1:30; (3) Hebrews 11:6; (4) James 1:5; (5) James 1:6; (6) Job 28:18; (7) Psalms 90:12; (8) James 1:17; (9) Psalms 111:10; (10) Proverbs 2:6; (11) Proverbs 2:6; (12) Proverbs 3:13; (13) Proverbs 3:15; (14) Proverbs 3:17; (15) Proverbs 3:18; (16) Proverbs 4:6; (17) John 15:16.

Prayers

For

Others

The preceding prayers of this book are personal prayers for you to use for your own life — healing prayers for your body, your emotions, and your mind. This final section of *Healing Prayers*, however, contains prayers for you to pray for others — intercessory prayers of physical, emotional, and mental healing for those you know and love.

The ministry of intercessory prayer is a vital and important process in which every believer can engage. When you become aware of the problems of other individuals, you may sometimes wonder what you can do for them.

Praying for a person in need is something that will bring real help, because through intercession you are "standing in the gap" for the one you care about. (See Ezek. 22:30.) God always honors your prayers for others. In fact, medical science confirms this. A recent article reports the finding of hospital researchers who studied what happens to patients recovering from surgery when they are prayed for. In almost every case, those who were prayed for (even those who did not know someone was praying for them) recovered from surgery much more quickly and fully than those who were not prayed for at all.

Paul's first letter to Timothy calls you to the ministry of intercession: "Therefore I exhort first of all that supplications, prayers, intercessions, giving of thanks be made for all" (1 Tim. 2:1, NKJV). Paul concludes this exhortation with these words, "For this is good and acceptable in the sight of God our Savior" (1 Tim. 2:3, NKJV).

This "good and acceptable" ministry of intercession is backed up by the power and intercession of the Holy Spirit, who: ". . .helps in our weaknesses. For we do not know what we should pray for as we ought, but the Spirit Himself makes intercession for us" (Rom. 8:26, NKJV).

The Holy Spirit is your Helper in all things, and He will lead you as you pray for others. In fact, He is your Intercessor, who "makes intercession for the saints according to the will of God" (Rom. 8:27, NKJV).

Keep this in mind as you pray the following Bible-based prayers for others. Remember and believe the prayer promises and healing promises of God's Word that are used, outlined, and discussed in the previous sections of this book. In the same way that God hears and answers your personal prayers of faith, He will hear and answer your prayers for others. He will respond to your faith-filled prayers by giving the needed healings to those you lift up to Him.

Paul frequently prayed mighty prayers of intercession for his fellow-believers. Several of these prayers are included in the New Testament and can be adapted for use in your own ministry of intercession and your personal prayer life as well. For example, Paul wrote: "For this reason I bow my knees to the Father of our Lord Jesus Christ, from whom the whole family in heaven and earth is named, that He would grant you, according to the riches of His glory, to be strengthened with might through His Spirit in the inner man, that Christ may dwell in you hearts through faith; that you, being rooted and grounded in love, may be able to comprehend with all the saints what is the width and length and depth and height — to know the love of Christ which passes knowledge; that you may be filled with all the fullness of God" (Eph. 3:14-19, NKJV).

Paul's prayer is our prayer for you as well. May God bless you as you endeavor to bless others through intercessory prayer.

100

Physical Healing for Another

A Prayer of Intercession for Physical Healing

Healing Promise: *"Pray for one another, that you may be healed"* (James 5:16, NKJV).

Healing Prayer: Heavenly Father, thank you for your healing mercy and for your desire to heal your children who are sick. I come to you now on behalf of _____, who suffers from _____. I ask you, Father, to heal _____ and to restore him/her to complete physical health.

I praise you for the many promises of your Word, which proclaim healing for those who are sick. Thank you for providing healing through the stripes of Jesus.[1] I believe your hands will make _____ whole because this is the promise of your Word.[2]

I take great joy in your promise that though the afflictions of the righteous may be many, you, Father, will deliver them out of them all.[3] You are the Lord that heals us.[4] Heal _____, O Lord God and I know he/she shall be healed. You are the Lord who is healing _____, for you forgive all of our iniquities and heal all our diseases.[5]

Father, I ask you to gird _____ with strength and make his/her way perfect.[6] Strengthen him/her according to the promises of your Word.[7] Thank you for Jesus, who took all our infirmities and carried all our diseases away.[8] Your Word says, Father, that with the stripes of Jesus we are healed.[9] Father, you have provided an open door of healing for us through Jesus Christ, who is the same yesterday, today and forever.[10]

Father God, you said to pray for one another, that we may be healed, and that the prayer of faith will save the sick and you will raise them up.[11] In faith, I bring _____ to you now, and I beseech you, Father, to raise him/her up. Send healing on the wings of your Spirit to him/her.[12] You have promised to be his/her Healer, Lord God. Do not permit this affliction to remain in his/her body.

I hope in you, Lord God, and I will ever praise you for your goodness.[13] Father, you are the God of all hope. I ask you to fill _____with all joy and peace in believing, that he/she may abound in hope, through the power of the Holy Spirit.[14] Thank you for being health to_____ and for healing him/her. Glory be to your name forever and ever. In Jesus' name I pray, Amen.[15]

References: (1) 1 Peter 2:24; (2) Job 5:18; (3) Psalms 34:19; (4) Exodus 15:26; (5) Psalms 103:3; (6) Psalms

18:32; (7) Psalms 119:28; (8) Matthew 8:17; (9) Isaiah 53:5; (10) Hebrews 13:8; (11) James 5:15-16; (12) Malachi 4:2; (13) Psalms 42:11; (14) Romans 15:13; (15) John 16:23-24.

101

Emotional Healing for Another

A Prayer for the Healing of
Another Person's Emotions

Healing Promise: *"The Spirit of the Lord is upon me, because he hath anointed me to preach the gospel to the poor; he hath sent me to heal the broken-hearted, to preach deliverance to the captives, and the recovering of sight to the blind, to set at liberty them that are bruised"* (Luke 4:18).

Healing Prayer: Father, I thank you that you heal the broken-hearted, you deliver the captives, and you set those free who have been bruised.[1] Your Word assures me that you will bind up our wounds and your hands will make us whole.[2]

As I pray to you now, Father, I claim these promises from your Word on behalf of _____, who needs healing for his/her heart and emotions.

Thank you that all the promises of your mighty Word are yes and amen in Christ Jesus.[3] Father, _____'s heart has been bruised, and I ask you to heal his/her heart and help him/her to walk in the freedom and liberty with which Christ has set him/her free.[4]

Help _____ to regain a merry heart, Lord God, for a merry heart will be good like a medicine, and your medicine is the best medicine of all.[5] Jesus has borne the griefs of your children, and carried their sorrows, and with His stripes your children are healed, Father.[6] Through faith, therefore, I claim this promise on behalf of _____, Father, and ask that you bring total healing and restoration to his/her heart, emotions, and soul.[7]

When _____ is cast down and upset, Father, help him/her to hope in you, and to praise you for helping him/her to smile again.[8] Help _____ to do as David did and encourage himself/herself in you.[9]

Heal _____, O Lord God, and he/she will be healed. Be his/her praise.[10] Thank you for the ongoing ministry of the Lord Jesus Christ, whom you anointed to heal the broken-hearted and to proclaim deliverance to the captives.[11] Father, I express faith to you now that this is happening in the life of _____, and I ask you to help him/her experience your joy as he/she receives your healing for his/her broken-heartedness.[12] Renew his/her strength as he/she waits upon you.[13] Thank you so much.

Help _____
to believe and to experience the fullness of
your promise that the old things are passed
away and you are making all things new in
his/her life.[14] Father, I believe that, with your
help, _____ will walk in
wholeness and renewal from this time
forward. Thank you for all that you've done
and are doing for him/her.

Thank you for hearing and answering
my prayer, Father. In Jesus' mighty name I
pray, Amen.[15]

References: (1) Luke 4:18; (2) Job 5:18; (3) 2 Corinthians
1:20; (4) Galatians 5:1; (5) Proverbs 17:22; (6) Isaiah 53:5;
(7) Psalms 23:3; (8) Psalms 42:5; (9) 1 Samuel 30:6; (10)
Jeremiah 17:14; (11) Luke 4:18; (12) John 16:24; (13)
Isaiah 40:31; (14) 2 Corinthians 5:17; (15) John 15:16.

102

Mental Healing for Another

*A Prayer for the Mental Healing
of Another Person*

Healing Promise: *"For God hath not given us the spirit of fear; but of power, and of love, and of a sound mind"* (2 Tim. 1:7).

Healing Prayer: Dear God, thank you that you have given all of your children the spirit of power, love, and a sound mind in place of all mental afflictions, including fear.[1] I humbly ask you to fulfill your Word in the life of _____ and to remove all mental disturbances from his/her life. Let the sound mind that has been given to him/her through Christ, function perfectly in him/her. I know you are not the author of confusion, but of peace, and I ask you to impart great peace to his/her mind.[2] Thank you for the wonderful promises of your Word, Father.

Help _____, Lord God, and I know that he/she will not be confounded any longer. Help him/her to trust in you, Father, and with your help to set his/her face like a flint and never to be ashamed.[3] Heal him/her, and bind up his/her wounds.[4] Thank you for the wonderful peace that Jesus imparts to him/her — a peace that the world cannot give or ever take away.[5]

Help _____ to draw near to you, Father, for I realize that, as he/she does, you will draw near to him/her with your healing presence. This will enable _____ to have clean hands and a pure heart and to be free from all double-mindedness.[6] Thank you, Father. Help him/her to humble himself/herself in your sight, Lord God, and, as he/she does so, I realize that you will lift him/her up.[7]

As I pray to you, Lord God, I am fully persuaded that neither death nor life, nor angels, nor principalities, nor powers, nor things present, nor things to come, nor height, nor depth, nor any other creature, shall be able to separate me from your love, which I've found in Christ Jesus my Lord.[8] I ask you to impart this same confidence in your ever-present love to _____. Thank you, Father.

By your mercies, Father, I ask you to help _____ present his/her body, now, a living sacrifice, holy and acceptable unto you, for this is his/her reasonable service of worship to you. Help him/her never to be conformed to this world but to be fully transformed by the renewing of his/her mind, so that he/she will always be able to prove your good, acceptable, and perfect will for his/her life.[9]

Thank you, Father, for your truth which truly makes _____ free in his/her mind.[10] Be merciful and minister to_____, Father, and help him/her to call upon you, for your Word declares that whoever calls upon you will be delivered.[11]

Deliver _____ from evil,[12] Father, and from every attack of the enemy. I ask, in the name of Jesus, that he/she be delivered from every hindering mental stronghold in his/her life and that those strongholds be cast down and no longer have any force or effect in his/her life,[13] as you deliver and heal him/her, Lord God. Overthrow these strongholds, Father, and set him/her totally free.

From this day forward I pray that _____ will be free from all mental problems, and that he/she will live strong in you, Lord God, and in the power of your might.[14] Thank you, Father. In the mighty name of Jesus I pray, Amen.[15]

References: (1) 2 Timothy 1:7; (2) 1 Corinthians 14:33; (3) Isaiah 50:7; (4) Psalms 147:3; (5) John 14:27; (6) James 4:8; (7) James 4:10; (8) Romans 8:38-39; (9) Romans 12:1-2; (10) John 8:32; (11) Joel 2:32; (12) Matthew 6:13; (13) 2 Corinthians 10:5; (14) Ephesians 6:10; (15) John 16:23-24.